Suicide Loss Grief;

A GUIDE TO PUSHING THROUGH

By Tamara Leigh

Table of Contents

INTRODUCTION 1

Group Participant Guidelines 7

WEEK 1.. 9
Welcome/What Is Suicide?

WEEK 2.. 27
Stages of Suicide Loss Grief/Shock

WEEK 3.. 37
Denial/Anger/Crying

WEEK 4.. 47
Fear/Anxiety/Silence

WEEK 5.. 59
Guilt/Shame/Notes

WEEK 6.. 71
Mourning/Memories/Self-Esteem

WEEK 7.. 83
Crisis of Faith/Trusting God

WEEK 8.. 97
Patience/Hopelessness, Hope

WEEK 9.. 107
The Questions

WEEK 10.. 117
Trauma/PTSD/Depression

WEEK 11.. 135
The Body/Taking Care of Yourself

WEEK 12.. 145
Rejection/Regret/Relief

WEEK 13.. 159
Love and Grace/Forgiveness/Joy and Happiness

WEEK 14.. 171
Stigma/Secondary Wounds

WEEK 15.. 191
Pushing Through/Laughter/New Normal/Gratitude

WEEK 16.. 207
The Journey/Closure/After Grief

SURVIVING THE TENDER DAYS AND HOLIDAYS 219

MOTHER'S/FATHER'S DAY AFTER LOSING A CHILD 227

INTRODUCTION

*Let us then approach God's throne of grace with confidence,
so that we may receive mercy and find grace to help us
in our time of need.*
~ Hebrews 4:16 (NIV – New International Version)

I never thought much about the word suicide. I felt it was a word that applied to anyone but me. But in 2016, I became very aware of this word. My boyfriend died by suicide. After his death, I learned he had suffered for many years with mental pain from the wounds of his childhood, military, life, and PTSD. I never knew before his death that he was in pain.

So why did I write this publication?

After my boyfriend died, I was in so much emotional pain. I called my counselor and asked where the nearest group meeting was for people who had lost someone to suicide. She said there was no such thing in our area. I wanted to scream. I needed to be with people who KNEW what I was feeling. I felt isolated.

I was in shock. I was in silence. I was alone.

I live in an area that is home to one of the largest military installations in our country. With so many veteran suicides a day, why was there not a place for us suicide loss survivors to go? I had no place to turn to that offered specific help for what I was feeling after losing the man I love to suicide.

"Blessed are those who mourn, for they will be comforted."
~ Matthew 5:4 (NIV)
(Unless stated otherwise, all scriptures in this handbook
are taken from the NIV.)

1

I have experienced other types of grief: loss of ability to have a child, losing my mother, losing my brother, loss of jobs, marriage ending, loss of favorite relatives and a dear friend. Suicide loss is a grief unlike any other. After being on this suicide loss grief journey, I know all about the stigmas, the stares, the accusations, the silence, the unanswered questions, and how suicide turns your life completely around.

After the numbness, shock, denial, anger, and so many other unexpected emotions were fading, I felt God calling me to help others. My hope is that other people will have a resource and group to turn to, so that they may not feel as hopeless and alone as I did when my boyfriend died. There is healing in our Heavenly Father. I am an example that there is hope. I promise that healing does come. And I promise your light will shine again.

This publication is from my heart. It isn't from a professional counselor's point of view or based on scientific data. I am a gal who has been journeying through suicide loss grief with no map to guide me. And I created this 16-week guide so others could understand that we are not alone in what we feel after losing our loved one to suicide.

I have a degree in physical education, which has equipped me with the understanding of how the human body reacts to what I have experienced with suicide loss grief. I have read so many books on suicide and suicide loss, searched the internet through and through for any information I could find dealing with suicide loss grief, joined social media groups that have other folks experiencing the same pains as myself, and lived through the pains of losing someone I love to suicide. This publication is a cumulation of all I have felt, learned, and seen since the day my boyfriend took his own life.

Coming to a group – finding a safe place to talk, share, and listen – is a very important step towards healing. I am glad you are here to start your journey towards restoration. We are all connected in this suicide loss grief. I hope you will feel the safe embrace of this group and this publication.

Therefore encourage one another and build each other up,
just as in fact you are doing.
~ 1 Thessalonians 5:11

I suggest getting a journal or two for this grief journey. Each week includes opportunities to journal through the process. If you are anything like me, your emotions are all over the place right now. There are feelings of loss, emptiness, and sadness. Then you feel numb, you cry, and you want to be left alone. Anger comes. Or you feel like screaming. You hide from others because of shame and guilt. But you don't laugh anymore. There is no joy in the things that used to bring you joy. Tears come for no reason. Writing through your emotions can help you process as you live through each day, one at a time.

This is a very unique grief. As we search for the answers to all of our unanswered questions, we will grow to accept all that we don't understand. Every step of our grief journey brings new hope, healing, peace, and a bigger heart of compassion and love. I pray that, through this publication, you will grow in ways you never imagined; that you heal; and that you realize just how strong you are. Even though the times can be tough and messy, just know: you are never alone.

Praise be to the God and Father of our Lord Jesus Christ,
the Father of compassion and the God of all comfort,
who comforts us in all our troubles,
so that we can comfort those in any trouble
with the comfort we ourselves receive from God.
~ 2 Corinthians 1:3-4

You may have seen a semicolon used as an image associated with suicide. As defined by Merriam-Webster Dictionary, the semicolon is *"a punctuation mark (;) indicating a pause, typically between two main clauses, that is more pronounced than that indicated by a comma."* So our loved one's life led up to the semicolon – then the pause – and now, our life is after the semicolon. We don't just get there automatically, though. We have to Push Through so we don't get stuck in that "pause" – until we are beyond the semicolon.

Some people who have attempted suicide get a tattoo of a semicolon. Some people will get a semicolon tattoo to signify the memory of their loved one who died by suicide, in a color that represents a certain type of suicide causation. (For example, turquoise blue represents suicide due to PTSD.) You will find the semicolon on the cover of this book. It simply means: **my story is not over yet.**

For me, there was a pause in life when my boyfriend died by suicide. Now my life is more pronounced, and I will continue to Push Through. The healing comes. You, too, can Push Through this grief journey of suicide loss with God's healing and help.

Let Your Light Shine,
Tamara

Blog: hoperunpray.live
Email: pushthrough416@gmail.com
Facebook: fb.me/SuicideLossGrief
Instagram: SuicideLossGriefPushingThrough

Group Participant Guidelines

Your primary goal while attending this group is to heal from the trauma of your loss due to suicide. Because we want everyone to be comfortable and to feel free to share whatever is on their mind and heart, we ask that you adhere to the following guidelines:

- Be respectful towards yourself and others.
- What is said in the group stays within the group. Never repeat anything, as discussing what is heard/shared can cause great distress and bring undue emotional, legal, or physical harm. If it is discovered that someone is talking/sharing outside the group, that person will no longer be welcome.
- Be sensitive to others' loss and experience. We all have different journeys in suicide loss grief.
- Be open to sharing your experience, and encourage others to share theirs. Please refrain from giving advice.
- Don't compare losses. No suicide loss method is greater than another suicide loss method. Suicide loss is not greater than any other type of loss; it is just different.
- In this environment, everyone is free to express feelings, to share experiences and successful milestones, to laugh, and to cry.
- Limit your time of sharing to allow others time to share. There is healing in talking.
- Be open to learning, healing, and Pushing Through. Commit to attending, participating, and doing suggested "homework."
- If feeling offended with Facilitator(s) or another member of the group, speak to them in private and work through it.
- Group is volunteer-led and is not a counseling service. Facilitator(s) are committed to helping others heal and Push Through in the suicide loss grief process.

Confidentiality Policy Agreement

I recognize the importance of confidentiality and agree to abide by the Group Participant Guidelines.

_____

Name (Printed)

_____   _____

Signature   Date

WEEK 1

Welcome
What Is Suicide?

WELCOME! Being here is an important step in your healing. It was brave and courageous for you to step out and share this very unique and unknown grief with others. Coming to a group – finding a safe place where you can talk, listen, and share – is a very important step in healing.

This group is for people who have experienced a loss to suicide. This group is also for those who have lost someone to drug overdose, as these types of grief are so much alike. In both cases, your loved one is gone because they made a choice. There's ongoing debate: is overdose a suicide? Could it be another form of suicide? Possibly. For this healing process, we will include overdose death with suicide loss grief, even though it will not be mentioned separately in most of the publication.

Two are better than one,
because they have a good return for their labor:
If either of them falls down, one can help the other up.
But pity anyone who falls and has no one to help them up. . . .
Though one may be overpowered, two can defend themselves.
A cord of three strands is not quickly broken.
~ Ecclesiastes 4:9-10,12

We are all connected in suicide loss grief: what happens to one of us happens to all of us. Think of this group as a safe embrace. You can cry. You can laugh. You can be angry. You can be sad. You can share and talk with others who understand. You can be hugged and hug others. You will realize you are not alone in what you feel and think.

Please be considerate and respectful. What is shared here stays here. Each of us already feels betrayed by our loved one, and we don't want to be fearful that what we share in this group will be shared with others outside this group. Respect one another. Don't interrupt someone when they are sharing. Please don't give advice unless someone asks for it.

I hope this group will provide a self-embrace for you personally. Even if you are surrounded by others in this group who have suffered this same loss, the journey is yours alone. In healing, there is peace. We must keep Pushing Through this grief so that peace will reveal itself in our healing. I love this quote:

We can never obtain peace in the outer world
until we make peace with ourselves.
~the Dalai Lama

Being here – choosing to work through your grief – is a first step towards healing. Towards peace.

"Blessed are those who mourn, for they will be comforted."
~ Matthew 5:4

It is okay not to be okay. It's okay to mourn and grieve in whatever way you want to. There are no rules. Do what, how, and when the way you want or need to. This is your journey.

There will be many moments when you feel this is a lonely journey. You are not alone in this feeling of loneliness. Each of us in this group feels the same way. But, by being here, you are surrounded by others who understand how you feel. Take comfort in knowing that here, you are understood.

We all will experience and express this grief differently. It is an individual journey that doesn't come with a road map. One step at a time. Allow for stops along the way. It's an unfamiliar path, so move with caution. If you discover you have made a wrong turn, STOP. Reassess. Then begin again, perhaps in a new direction. Expect to have days of three steps forward, one step back. There will be setbacks; I like to call them "aftershocks." Expect them. One moment at a time, one day at a time, until your loss is a reality.

There is no timetable for your grief. And your grief journey may travel differently than your spouse, or sibling, or best friend, or family member. Stay in your lane. Stay on your path! Let them do their journey, and you do yours.

Praise be to the God and Father of our Lord Jesus Christ,
the Father of compassion and the God of all comfort,
who comforts us in all our troubles,
so that we can comfort those in any trouble
with the comfort we ourselves receive from God.
~ 2 Corinthians 1:3-4

God is here to comfort each of us. We need to surrender our grief to Him. Letting go will be key during this grief journey. I suggest that you let go of the "What If's and embrace the "What Is." Surrender to "What Is" – the present – the here and now!

We know there is no future in living in the past. We can't change the past. We can only live in the right-now – and we can have hope and dreams for tomorrow.

Think of this analogy. A car's front windshield is large, so we can see clearly what is ahead of us. There is also a rearview mirror in the top middle part of that windshield for us to glance into – to glance at where we have been and see what is behind us. We can't stare into that rearview mirror for long. If we do, we will not see what is in front of us or where we are going. We will not be able to steer well, and more than likely, we will wreck.

Stay in the present, look ahead to the future, and only glance into the past from time to time to remember the lessons from where you have been.

The suicide loss grief process is messy for us. It seems to feel like a raging sea most of the time. The waves come and go. One day, the wave will be a tsunami, knocking us completely off our feet. And some days, the waves are so gentle that they barely break. Unpredictable and messy!

In suicide loss grief, rational explanations and logical conclusions are not present. There is a constant state of unsettledness. We find that we receive little comfort from others, and we are confused by so many unanswered questions. Just as our loved one who took their life was not rational in their actions, now our lives seem to be the same: irrational. Not much makes sense right now, and we are uncertain that anything will ever make sense again.

There will be triggers that you encounter. What is a trigger exactly? As defined by Dictionary.com, a "trigger warning" is *"a stated warning that the content of a text, video, etc. may upset or offend some people, especially those who have previously experienced a related trauma."* You may not recognize what a trigger is at first. The trigger can be a smell, a song, a movie, a location, a memory, a person, a picture, etc. These triggers will take you back to the moment you found out. Triggers can also be positive, taking you to a favorite memory between you and your loved one.

Expect triggers. The goal is to keep Pushing Through this grief. Do not get frozen in the process. It is an ebb and flow process, like the ocean waves.

Try not to let grief define who you are. Just as "suicide" is not the definition of who our loved one was, suicide loss grief is not the definition of who we are. It is a part of us – a chapter of our life. But it is not our whole book. Let's not give grief any power in our life. If we do give power to grief, then grief will define us – and that hurt interferes with our healing.

It is true: death is permanent. But our suicide loss grief is NOT permanent. I know it doesn't feel possible right now, but life does get more bearable. Don't be dismayed; peace will come, in time. We must Push Through this grief journey.

We can subconsciously delay the grief process. Grief takes longer if you stay too busy, if you mask with alcohol and/or drugs, or if you get yourself into any unhealthy vice. Avoidance of our grief delays the process of healing. There are no shortcuts in grief.

There may be things out of our control that can have a part in delaying the grief process. For example, the medical examiner's report can take a while for completion, due to the death being a suicide. Or there was an investigation of the death. Or the funeral home did not release the body when we thought it should be released. Or, like me, you weren't allowed to attend the funeral of your loved one. Maybe your family has divided due to your loved one's death being by suicide, as the blame game is usually in full force.

We have no control over the trauma, shock, denial, or other reactions that can delay the grief process, but we can control how we respond. We must move right through the middle of the grief to Push Through.

As much as you may not want it to be true, grief will change you. We have no control over this change. It just happens. But, the change doesn't have to be for the worse. Good can come from this grief. You may gain new friendships. You may learn a new skill. A new passion may be revealed. A hidden "gift" will emerge.

What changes may surprise you. Friendships that were not true will fade away, which is a good thing – even though it will make you sad that the friendship ended. Your heart may break, but your heart will also grow bigger with love and compassion.

One day you will realize that there is a new awakening, even among the gray skies.

SUICIDE

Suicide is "the act of intentionally causing one's own death." (*Stedman's Medical Dictionary*, 28th ed.)

I never thought I would ever have to understand or deal with the word "suicide." I ignorantly thought it was a word that only applied to crazy people. Boy, have I learned a lot. What is suicide? How does a person get to that point in their life? Why? Is there no help for people? Why not?

Suicide is not a natural death.

With suicide, the grief process is longer due to unanswered questions, guilt, anger, regret, shame, and silence. The shock multiplies the loss. Your loved one made the choice to end their life. This is very hard to accept. They made the choice to leave, to end their pain. In all other forms of death, the person does not choose for their life to end. A person doesn't choose to have cancer and die. A person doesn't choose to have a massive heart attack and die. We don't question when an older person passes away at 90 years old.

There is one thing that really bothers me when others are talking about suicide. It may not be such a sore spot for you, but it is for me: the words *"committed suicide."* The word "committed" has a lot of negative associations – for example, *"committed adultery."* Or a person is "committed" to a mental institution. Society automatically assumes a person goes to hell when they die by suicide. Nowhere in the Bible does it state this. (More on suicide and faith in a later week's discussion.) Suicide is not an "unpardonable sin," as some people claim, and it is not a crime. Please try to say *"died by suicide"* instead of *"committed suicide."* Or *"died as a result of mental illness."* Or *"died due to PTSD."*

Suicide divides more than it unites. Families divide due to blame, guilt, jealousy, or financial burden. However, suicide does unite us with others who have the same grief journey. The bonds we form with others who have experienced suicide loss grief are unbreakable. We will also draw closer to God with this grief. And, in time, we learn that it is only through Him that we can and will have peace and healing.

We must make sure that we take extra care of ourselves, because our wounds are so raw and deep for an extended period of time. Self-care needs to be a priority in this journey.

While doing some reading in my desire to understand what I was experiencing in my grief, I found a quote in the book *A Passage Through Grief: A Recovery Guide* by Barbara Baumgardner that has meant a lot to me:

> *Suicide – Brings the survivors into the torment*
> *the deceased was trying to escape from.*
> ~ Anonymous

This quote made me realize I was not crazy in my grief. It also gave me a sense of understanding about what my boyfriend had been experiencing. My heart of compassion grew with this quote, and it seems to continue to ring true.

Suicide may have been an act of peace for our loved one. Rest in emotional and mental balance had been void for them. This was the only way they could think of to find peace and rest. They are no longer at odds with the world, with others, with circumstances, with their past, or with their Self. Prior to the suicide act, they may have been neutral and detached. They may even have seemed at peace. Their appearance of peace before their death may have been because they had made the decision to end their life. They knew the pain was coming to an end soon.

My loved one's suicide was an action intended to put an end to his suffering and pain, not to cause mine. He didn't do this TO me. I think he felt he had no hope for the future and was in total despair. Obviously, he could not bear his burden any longer. He was not selfish. He was not a coward. He was not weak. He felt he was a burden. His state of mind was no longer rational.

If anything, in his thinking, he felt that he was removing a burden – himself – from the lives of his loved ones, which was selfless from his irrational perspective. This is the rationale that I have discovered. My boyfriend was not selfish, and his goal was not to cause me or anyone else any pain.

Our loved one was in mental anguish. We could not see it with our eyes. It is possible they felt that no one cared enough to be interested in them, or they felt they had no network of support. Maybe they had no idea how to get rid of their pain. Maybe they felt they had no one to talk to. Taking their own life became the only way they could think of to end the pain.

These are the thoughts they had, not the way we feel about them or how we viewed them. Our perception of them is not the perception they had of themselves or what they thought our perception was of them. We look at their suicide as irrational. It doesn't make sense to us because we are looking at their choice through the lens of rational thinking.

It is often said that our loved one's suicide is a permanent solution to a temporary problem. We see suicide that way. Our loved one did not. We must accept what our loved one felt and thought. We can't understand where they were in their need for peace and rest. Let's have compassion for our loved one.

Suicide is irrational in our minds.

Suicide does not bring us peace.

Suicide turns our life into hell on earth.

There are always two parties to a death,
the person who dies and survivors who are bereaved. . . .
and in the apportionment of suffering,
the survivor takes the brunt.
~Arnold Toynbee

TYPES OF SUICIDE

There are four types of suicide, according to French sociologist Émile Durkheim. These four types of suicide are based on the degrees of imbalance of two social forces: social integration and moral regulation. (Kenneth Thompson, *Émile Durkheim*)

According to Durkheim, your loved one's suicide could be characterized by one of these or a combination:

Egoistic – *He/she does not feel connected to society and feels that he/she has no place in the world. He/she feels total isolation from the social group they had previously been a part of. There is a last-ditch resort of depression and isolation. Egoistic is commonly found in unmarried, military, and/or veterans who have not managed to reintegrate back into society or previous environment.*

Altruistic – *This is the opposite of egoistic. He/she has high levels of integration with society. He/she is social with others. He/she is known as the life of the party. He/she has high energy levels. He/she does not appear to have any problems or issues in life. This is the person whose choice of suicide is the most surprising.*

Anomic – *Comes from chaos and confusion, especially from social and economic upheaval. This occurs when the rules on how to behave with one another are breaking down and individuals do not know where they fit or how to behave. Social norms are lacking. This type can happen with extreme changes in economics. A person may have lost all their wealth (example: stock market crash).*

Fatalistic – *This is the opposite of anomic. There is no chaos or confusion, but excessive social restraint. A person may die by suicide on their way to prison, by cop, or to avoid an arranged marriage.*

It seems as if depression is a root of suicide. Depression stems from fear and anger: there is fear that a need will go unmet, and fear leads to anger. Depression = anger turned inward.

Substance abuse usually plays a part in depression and suicidal thoughts, and self-abuse often plays a part in suicide. Self-abuse comes in different forms like self-mutilation, overeating, too much exercise, alcohol/drugs, or other unhealthy patterns. My boyfriend was obsessed with the "perfect" body. I thought he was just taking really good care of himself.

The following are possible motivations for suicide: living with hopelessness, feelings of alienation, losing a job, feelings of failure and inadequacy, problems at work, feeling psychologically overwhelmed, guilt, losing a child or other loved one, desiring to leave problems behind, financial issues, seeking reunification with another in the afterlife, shame, the ending of a marriage, feeling like a burden, mental illness, physical pain, relational issues, or a combination of any of these. The list of motivations for suicide can go on and on. There is never a single motivation for suicide. We will never truly know every reason why our loved one took their life.

Hope deferred makes the heart sick . . .
~ Proverbs 13:12

SUICIDE FACTS

Suicide is the 10th leading cause of death in the US for all ages. (CDC – Centers for Disease Control)

Suicides per day in the US: 129. (AFSP – American Foundation for Suicide Prevention)

There is one death by suicide in the US every 12 minutes. (CDC)

Suicides per day in the world: 3000. (WHO – World Health Organization)
*This equals 1,095,000 suicide deaths a year in the world.

Depression affects 20%-25% of Americans ages 18+ in a given year. (CDC)

Only half of all Americans experiencing an episode of major depression receive treatment. (NAMI – National Alliance on Mental Illness)

Females experience depression at roughly 2 times the rate of men. (SMH – Society & Mental Health)

Depression is the leading cause of disability worldwide. (SAVE – Suicide Awareness Voices of Education)

80%-90% of people who seek treatment for depression are treated successfully using therapy and/or medication. (TADS – Treatment for Adolescents with Depression Study)

The highest suicide rates in the US are among Whites, American Indians, and Alaska Natives. (SAVE)

There can be up to 32 immediate suicide loss survivors for each suicide. (CDC)

An estimated quarter million people each year become suicide loss survivors. (AAS – American Association of Suicidology)

There is one suicide for every estimated 25 suicide attempts. (CDC)

There is one suicide for every estimated 4 suicide attempts in the elderly. (CDC)

Suicide is the 2nd leading cause of death in the world for those aged 15-24 years. (CDC)

Suicide among males is 4 times higher than among females. Male deaths represent 79% of all US suicides. (CDC)

Females are more likely than males to have had suicidal thoughts. (CDC)

Females attempt suicide 3 times as often as males. (CDC)

Firearms are the most commonly used method of suicide among males (51%). (CDC)

Poisoning is the most common method of suicide for females. (CDC)

1 in 100,000 children ages 10-14 die by suicide each year. (NIMH – National Institute of Mental Health)

7 in 100,000 youth ages 15-19 die by suicide each year. (NIMH)

12.7 in 100,000 young adults ages 20-24 die by suicide each year. (NIMH)

The prevalence of suicidal thoughts, suicidal planning, and suicide attempts is significantly higher among adults aged 18-29 than among adults aged 30+. (CDC)

Suicide is the 4th leading cause of death for adults ages 18-65. (CDC)

The highest increase in suicide is in males 50+ (30 per 100,000). (CDC)

Suicide rates for females are highest among those aged 45-54 (9 per 100,000). (CDC)

Suicide rates for males are highest among those aged 75+ (36 per 100,000). (CDC)

Suicide rates among the elderly are highest for those who are divorced or widowed. (SMH)

Suicide claims more lives per year than war, murder, and natural disasters combined. (AFSP)

Amount of people directly impacted by a suicide: minimum 32 per suicide. US: 4,129/day. Worldwide: 96,000/day. (SAVE)

It is shocking that 35,040,000 people per year are directly impacted by a suicide! That is a lot of hurting people. "Directly impacted" is not just the person's loved ones or friends; it can also include the co-workers, neighbors, community, or those who knew the person professionally as their dentist, landlord, doctor, accountant, mailman, investment counselor, or their own clients.

VETERANS

According to the VA (Veterans Administration), there are over 20 veteran suicides a day. Of all the suicide deaths, 18% are veterans. I personally don't believe this. I believe the number is higher. I believe the government does not give accurate numbers for this statistic.

The VA did a report which showed a total of 20.6 military suicides every day. Of those, 16.8 were veterans and 3.8 were active-duty service members, guardsmen, and reservists. That amounts to 6,132 veterans and 1,387 service members who died by suicide in one year.

Currently, there are 800 million people grieving a loss by suicide. And you are one of those. You are a survivor of suicide loss grief. You are surviving!

WAVES OF GRIEF

I like to compare this life-changing grief journey to the waves in the ocean. The waves crash big or small, and they ebb and flow. Over and over.

In the book *Silent Grief: Living in the Wake of Suicide* by Christopher Lukas and Henry N. Selden, the ocean waves are described like this:
~ *1st wave: shock, denial, helplessness, relief, blame*
~ *2nd wave: anger, guilt, shame, anxiety*
~ *3rd wave: depression, low self-esteem*
~ *4th wave: psychological and physical problems, propensity towards suicide itself, suicide ideation*

You may not experience each aspect of these waves, but you will probably experience most of them. The cycles may not go in the order listed here. Don't be surprised if the wave cycles ebb and flow, or if the cycles are repeated. You will get knocked down, but you have to get back up – over and over – as you Push Through. We all understand and have been in the same spot you are. You are not alone.

HOMEWORK

1 – Has your overall perspective on life changed since your loved one's suicide? If yes, what do you perceive differently? How?

2 – Which of the types of suicide best describes your loved one's suicide? Or is it a combination of one or more types? Write down your thoughts on this "types of suicide" idea.

3 – Where are you currently with the Waves of Grief? Have you experienced any of the waves more than once? Grab your journal and write about it.

4 – Of the verses mentioned in group today, which is your favorite and why?

5 – Based on today's meeting, what would you like to say to your loved one? Write them a letter about how you feel.

Practical Encouragement

This week, go for a walk outside. Fresh air will help clear your thoughts and get the blood flowing through your body.

WEEK 2

Stages of Suicide Loss Grief
Shock

This week, we will discuss the stages of suicide loss grief and the shock experienced during suicide loss.

15 STAGES OF SUICIDE GRIEF

In 1969, Elizabeth Kübler-Ross wrote in her book *On Death and Dying* about the five stages of grief: denial, anger, bargaining, depression, acceptance. Some stages of suicide loss grief, like denial and anger, are the same as stages found with other types of grief. But it all looks different when there is a suicide. Suicide makes grief unpredictable, unique, and lonely.

Here is the list that I created based on the stages of grief I experienced during my grieving period of suicide loss. I have experienced other types of grief, but this grief due to loss by suicide is DIFFERENT. I'm not saying it is worse or greater than other griefs; it is just different.

1 – Shock
2 – Denial
3 – Need for Reason – The Questions - Why?
4 – Stigma/Accusations
5 – Guilt/Confusion/Shame
6 – Anger/Resentment
7 – Blame
8 – Despair/Hopelessness
9 – Depression/Sadness
10 – Isolation/Loneliness/Disconnection/Rejection
11 – Physical Symptoms of Distress
12 – Panic/Anxiety/Fear
13 – Sense of Relief
14 – Resistance of Return to Life/Setbacks/Triggers
15 – Acceptance/HOPE/Moving On (Pushing Through)

We will touch on each of these 15 stages in the weeks to come. Your grief journey may be a little different: you may not experience all the stages that I have come up with, or you may experience a stage that I don't have listed. You may pass through one more quickly than another. You may pass through one or all more than once. There is no order for the stages of suicide loss grief. However you are experiencing it, it is ok. You are not "losing it."

We in this group are with you, but your grief is personal and yours alone. No one can tell you how to grieve, how long to grieve, or what your grief is supposed to look like. It's messy, and we all must Push Through in our own way.

There is no doubt that our lives are forever changed by a loss due to suicide. There will be aspects of our lives that need to change if we want to find the healing we long for. In our grief, change and healing require three things: Acceptance, Forgiveness, and Compassion.

> *Finally, all of you, be like-minded, be sympathetic,*
> *love one another, be compassionate and humble.*
> ~ 1 Peter 3:8

Acceptance – We must accept what is. Right now, the "what is" for us is that our loved one died by suicide. We must deal with reality, even though we don't like the reality of our loved one being gone, of the suicide itself, and of our grief. The first step is to accept it, as it is true. Our loved one is gone. Our loved one made the choice to end their life. This grief is real. We must Push Through.

We need to create a space where healing can happen. Acceptance opens the door to fresh air, new energy, and new beginnings. Acceptance opens "self" to the present. We can't move forward if we are existing in the past.

28

Forgiveness – We need forgiveness in every aspect of our lives, but especially now, in our grief. If we don't forgive, we get stuck. We remain in the past. We stew in rage, anger, bitterness, and hurt. We must let go of what burdens us. We must release what hardens and constricts our hearts. Forgiveness is not an emotion, but a decision – a decision that takes time. Forgiveness is not an instant resolution. Be patient with yourself when processing forgiveness.

Then Peter came to Jesus and asked,
"Lord, how many times shall I forgive my brother or sister
who sins against me? Up to seven times?"
Jesus answered,
"I tell you, not seven times, but seventy-seven times."
~ Matthew 18:21-22

Forgiving does not equal forgetting. We will never forget our loved one. We will not forget the moment we found our loved one or were notified of the death. We will not forget the hurtful things said to us after the suicide. We will not forget the memories. We forgive our loved one for ending their life, and for the fact that we are now in this pain. We forgive others when they are not kind, or when they forget about us. We forgive ourselves – this is a huge step. We forgive in all areas that need forgiveness. Prayerfully, we will continue to forgive – and, in time, the pain from our loss will lessen and then disappear.

Compassion is *"sympathetic pity and concern for the sufferings or misfortunes of others"* (Lexico.com). Compassion is found through forgiveness and acceptance. In the act of compassion, our heart is able to expand, and we come to understand and accept others' actions and frailties.

In our grief, we want others to be compassionate towards us. We crave to have another to suffer with. It helps to have someone

29

understand what we are feeling and experiencing. That is why it is important to be in a group with others who have experienced a loss due to suicide. We "get it" and understand the path that each of us is on. We are all connected, we are all one in this, and we all show one another true compassion. We are all on the same path, even though our journeys are different from one another.

We think that others should show compassion to us during this time of loss, but as weird as it sounds, I became more compassionate to others during the suicide loss grief process.

I decided to show compassion to my boyfriend's parents when they did not allow me to be at his funeral, even though their decision kept me from grieving with others who loved him. I didn't know what their reason was, but I chose to have an understanding and compassionate heart towards them and the loss they felt. They had my boyfriend for 35 years as their son. I can't even imagine the pain they were experiencing. I chose to pray for them. I chose to forgive them for not wanting me to be at the funeral. I tried to be understanding towards his family and not take their decision personally.

Without the three steps of acceptance, forgiveness, and compassion, our hearts remain shut down and closed. We can't move forward. We remain in grief and heartbreak. These three steps may not come in order, as written here. They are not automatic; it takes time and conscious effort on our part to experience acceptance, forgiveness, and compassion. They are components of the road to healing.

I prayed from the very beginning for healing to come quickly and for my heart not to become hard in the process of healing. I felt that this grief had the opportunity to turn me into a stone-hard person in all things, especially in the affairs of the heart. I decided to love others. As difficult as it has been at times to truly love, I have made the effort to do so.

I still struggle with trust, even after years. Your struggle may be forgiveness, acceptance, moving forward, or loving others. We are all different and experience our grief and healing in our own ways.

I continue and always will continue to go through these steps of acceptance, forgiveness, and compassion. Don't get disheartened by me saying this. I just want you to know: it is a process we continually have to Push Through, and a process we may experience numerous times in this journey.

SHOCK

noun – a sudden or violent disturbance of the mind, emotions, or sensibilities (Dictionary.com); the feeling of being very surprised by something bad that happens unexpectedly (Macmillan Dictionary); the feeling of distress and disbelief that you have when something bad happens accidentally (Vocabulary.com)

verb – collide violently (Vocabulary.com); cause (someone) to feel surprised and upset, offend the moral feelings of, experience outrage (Lexico.com)

Shock, as both a noun and a verb, applies to this grief of suicide loss. The upsetting or surprising event is the suicide act itself.
A "sudden or violent disturbance of the mind, emotions, or sensibilities" describes my world after the realization that someone I love died by suicide. It has sometimes felt like an emotional earthquake with aftershocks – not to mention the violent physical shaking of how I fell to the ground and could not drag myself up off the pavement after I got the news. Oh yes, I felt surprised and distressed in the biggest way possible.

My emotions, my life, my body, my heart, my soul, my dreams, my world - they all collided violently the day I was told the news I had never dreamed I would hear about someone I love. *"He is no longer in pain, he is gone."* I was deeply shocked that he would end his own beautiful life. I was shocked that I hadn't known he was in so much pain.

I refused to believe he did it. No, it is not true, he wouldn't do that. Yelling at the top of my lungs – *NNNNOOOOOOO!!!!!!*

"Not him, he had everything going for him – his youth, his health, his family, his career, his looks, the promise of his future. Nope, he wouldn't do this."

"She had just graduated from college and was about to start her first career."

Denial comes with shock. Denial is that extra layer of protection while you process as much of the situation as you can. We may feel an internal refusal to deal with all the emotional consequences of the suicide act and the suicide loss grief. It becomes a conscious effort to deal with the emotions as, initially, we do not want to accept the truth. Denial will be discussed more in-depth in a week to come.

> *When I heard this, I tore both my garment and robe,*
> *plucked hair from both my head and my beard,*
> *and collapsed in shock!*
> ~ Ezra 9:3 (ISV – International Standard Version)

Shock is the first response to a traumatic event. It is automatic. It is physiological. We have no control over this reaction! It just happens to us. Shock protects you by keeping the full extent of devastation from hitting you all at once, so you don't lose your mind. The shock and numbness are necessary in the beginning. Our bodies are amazing: with shock, our brain provides a protective mechanism that allows a person to function until the gradual realization of the devastating news sets in. Shock numbs the psyche. As shock wears off, the process of accepting our devastation will begin.

More than likely, at some point in your grief, you will experience what is known as Fight or Flight (AKA acute stress response or hyperarousal), first described by Walter Bradford Cannon. When we experience something that is a threat to our survival – mental or physical, real or perceived – our body reacts automatically.

In simple terms, Fight or Flight means our body decides if it wants to put up a fight and deal with the stressful situation or if it wants to turn around and run from the stressful situation. In a more technical explanation of Fight or Flight, *"the sympathetic nervous system is activated. The adrenal gland produces secretions of catecholamine, norepinephrine and epinephrine. Other hormones in our body also play a part in how we react to stress; estrogen, testosterone, and cortisol. The neurotransmitters dopamine and serotonin also play a part in fight or flight."* (Walter Bradford Cannon – Istvan Berczi, University of Manitoba). This is psychological and cannot be controlled.

When a person is experiencing shock, the body reacts physiologically. Possible reactions may be any of the following: increased or decreased heart rate, blood pressure or breathing, anxiety, nausea, skin may be either pale or flush, or pupils may dilate (*Shock: Signs and Symptoms*, Healthline Media 2019). People experiencing shock may have each of these reactions or only a few of the symptoms. It is scary when this happens and tends to add to an already existing level of anxiety.

It is to be expected that a person will experience shock when a trauma has taken place. We have no control over this. It just happens in our physiological being, as it is a natural way for our body to deal with stress. Once you feel this happening, you may want to practice methods of calming and relaxing your body, to include breathing exercises.

How long a person experiences shock is varied. It could last for three hours or up to six weeks. For me, shock has had a way of "dropping in" from time to time along my journey. Rest assured: shock can happen anytime and is normal.

With suicide, shock is more intense. It is more intense due to the long list of unanswered questions and feelings of helplessness, anger, shame, guilt, rejection, and alienation. Our shock is wrapped up in the fact that we feel hurt and betrayed by our loved one. They didn't consult with us or turn to us for help before taking their life. We cannot believe it is real.

Your loved one has had the last say. We are in shock that there is no chance to say *"I love you"* one more time. No chance to say *"Goodbye."* No chance to say *"Forgive me"* or *"I forgive you."* No chance to make things "right." We have no control. Acceptance takes longer since there is regret and a lot of *"I wish I had . . ."*s.

The complete package – the mind, body, and spirit – must all adjust to shock. And the adjusting doesn't come all at once with mind, body, and spirit. The body may come first, with the mind following, then the spirit. Whatever the order is for you is okay. And while the shock may be strongest at the beginning of the process, it can also overlap into other stages, as well as return at different times in the future.

It is hard to think straight when you are in shock. You feel as if you are in a fog, or as if you are having a bad dream. You are numb and dumbfounded. You are without words and void of emotion. You are empty. Due to the fight or flight response in your body, you may experience muscle fatigue, dizziness, shortness of breath, nausea, or loss of appetite.

Try to calm down. There isn't much you can do to control this process, as your body knows what to do. Give it time. Typically, this is a short period of time. If this intense period of physical shock is extended, see a medical doctor or grief counselor.

HOMEWORK

1 – Use your journal and describe your experiences with acceptance, forgiveness, and compassion.

2 – What have you been in shock about the most? What has shock looked like for you – physically, mentally, emotionally, and spiritually?

3 – So far in your journey, which of the 15 stages of grief have you experienced? Which have been repeated? Are there other stages of your suicide grief – stages that you have experienced – that are not listed?

4 – Psalm 55:22 says, *"Cast your cares on the LORD and he will sustain you; he will never let the righteous be shaken."* Does this verse speak to you? How? Is there a verse you like better that gives you comfort?

5 – Be good to yourself this week. Find one thing you have been wanting to do and GO do it!

Practical Encouragement

Go for a walk three to five times this week for up to thirty minutes. Or go to a yoga class or go for a bike ride. Do some type of exercise you enjoy this week for up to thirty minutes.

WEEK 3

Denial
Anger
Crying

You will experience denial right after shock. They go hand in hand. You will be angry – angry at yourself, your loved one, God, everyone. And there will be lots of crying. You will cry and not even know why. Let's explore denial, anger and crying as they apply to our suicide loss grief.

DENIAL

noun – refusal to admit the truth or reality of something (Merriam-Webster Dictionary)

Denial comes with shock and is a common defense mechanism. It is an extra layer of protection, numbing our emotions while we process as much of our situation as we can. This is a temporary response that helps us get through the first phase or wave of our loss.

Denial stems from our feelings of hurt and betrayal by our loved one. It involves holding onto false beliefs. The following are examples of what denial may feel like for you:

"No, she wouldn't do this to me."
"He would not do this to himself on purpose."
"He really just took a vacation, and he didn't want me to go."
"He is in protective custody and can't be in touch with me yet."
"That really isn't her body that they found. It must be mistaken identity."

We just do not want to believe what is true. We will think of all kinds of scenarios or excuses about why or how our loved one took their own life:

"He didn't mean to."
"It was a mistake."
"He would never do that."
"The gun must have gone off accidentally."
"She didn't mean to take so many pills."
"She was so happy; somebody must have done this to her."
"Someone laced my son's drug with something fatal, and it killed him."

Try to accept the truth that your loved one is no longer here. Accepting the truth may come in baby steps, as we just find it so hard to understand or believe. And try not to deny that it was death by suicide. Denying the death was suicide actually gives more power to the devastation of suicide.

In this stage of denial, reaching out to a grief counselor or a pastor for help may be beneficial. Having someone listen to you and remind you of the truth will be healing. Try to be good to yourself by getting enough rest and staying physically active. Be patient with yourself and with this process.

Being in denial is automatic, just like shock. It's normal to go through this emotion. The feeling does pass. But it can also come back around again at another time in your grieving process, just like shock. If it does come back around, talk it out with someone who understands, or with a counselor. You have experienced a huge trauma, and you may experience various emotions multiple times.

ANGER

noun – a strong feeling of displeasure and usually of antagonism (Merriam-Webster Dictionary); the feeling people get when something unfair, painful, or bad happens (Cambridge Dictionary)

verb – to fill (someone) with anger; provoke anger in (Lexico.com)

Anger comes after denial. Yes, I felt strong "displeasure" and "antagonism." My loved one chose to leave this earth. I didn't want my loved one to go. Yes, I was filled with anger and other negative emotions in my process of accepting the truth.

You may have:

~ anger (rage) at your loved one for abandoning you
*"I walked by that container that holds my husband's ashes, and I
	yelled at the container many times."*

~ anger (rage) at others when you feel they are accusing you, blaming you for the suicide
"Did you not see the signs?"
"Why didn't you get her help?"

~ anger (rage) at someone you feel is responsible for the death
"No way he did this to himself; someone else killed him."
"His wife made him so mad that he did this to himself."

~ anger (rage) at yourself for letting it happen or for not stopping it
*"I should have taken her to rehab one more time; if I had, she
	would be here today."*
"Why didn't I do a wellness check on him?"

~ anger (rage) at God for allowing it to happen, for taking your loved one from you, and for your uncertainty about whether your loved one is in hell
"Why did God take my loved one?"
"What did I do that was so bad that God would do this to me?"
"I am mad at you, God."

You may not even be sure what you are angry about exactly, but you know something is "wrong." You may feel guilty because of the angry feelings you have. Due to the guilt, you may remain silent about your anger. Or, you may find yourself becoming more vocal. There may be bursts of anger that are physical, like screaming at the top of your lungs in your backyard. You may lash out at others verbally because of your anger, like yelling at your best friend for no warranted reason.

There may be other emotions and physical reactions that are a result of your anger. You may experience anxiety or panic attacks, confusion, flashbacks from the event, fear, chest pains, breathing problems, eating disturbances, sleep issues, or day-to-day function disturbances. If anger becomes a negative outlet – if you start hurting yourself or others – please seek medical help. We do not want to hurt anyone in our anger. Anger is a natural emotion and it is ok to experience it, but it should not come across in any negative behavior to ourselves or others.

There is a physiological effect that our bodies may experience in processing anger. The body may take over in a way commonly known as "blackout anger," which is a disorder called intermittent explosive disorder (IED).

According to the Mayo Clinic, *"IED involves repeated, sudden episodes of impulsive, aggressive, violent behavior or angry verbal outbursts in which a person reacts grossly out of proportion to the situation."* IED can consist of *"rage, irritability, increased energy, racing thoughts, tingling, tremors, palpitations, chest tightness."* A person has no thought of the consequences in *"temper tantrums, tirades, heated arguments, shouting, slapping, shoving or pushing, physical fights, property damage, and threatening or assaulting people or animals." "A person may feel a sense of relief and tiredness after the episode of IED. Later, [the person] may feel remorse, regret or embarrassment."* Often, the person may have no recollection of the anger outburst.

This doesn't happen just in grief. IED also happens in other situations where anger is present. If you experience IED, please seek medical help from a mental health professional. This is a disorder that needs immediate attention, due to the harmful side effects.

Our bodies may experience a certain amount of numbing in anger and denial. This is natural and normal. What we don't want to do is numb anger or pain with alcohol, drugs, or any other type of addictive outlet. Other numbing outlets could include overeating, throwing yourself into work, too much exercise, shopping sprees, too much sleep, or just too much of anything.

Usually, when a person is in the process of numbing, it isn't a conscious effort. It's almost as if the body and mind take over, trying to push off reality with the numbing process. I found myself in this situation when I became really busy with volunteering efforts. I was choosing a serving disposition to numb myself from the reality of losing my boyfriend; helping others was my method of pushing off truth and acceptance.

We should make a conscious effort if we see we are doing too much of anything. We should ask ourselves if we are numbing our emotions through this activity, or ask a good friend or family member if they recognize that we are doing something too much. If we find ourselves numbing too much or in an unhealthy way – if this is something you can't solve on your own – seek the help of a professional.

"In your anger do not sin":
Do not let the sun go down while you are still angry . . .
~ Ephesians 4:26

We can have anger – it's what we do with that anger that matters.

Well, what can you do with your anger?

Accept that this isn't "you" and that you are adjusting to a new normal.

41

"I am forever changed by my best friend's suicide. I miss her. She was my only sidekick and I want her back."

You can express your anger. Don't hold it in, and make sure you are expressing it in non-destructive ways. When talking or sharing with others, try using an *"I feel"* statement followed by your emotion: *"I feel angry that you refused to acknowledge that my daughter died."* You may want to go for a walk, hit a punching bag, go swimming, write in your journal, go do some endorphin-releasing exercise like fast walking or swimming, or take up a new hobby that will let you vent your anger in a non-destructive way.

After anger, there may be an opportunity for forgiveness. Someone doesn't have to ask you for forgiveness for you to grant it. Forgive yourself and others. Forgive your loved one who took their life. In forgiveness, there is peace. Where peace exists, anger can subside.

> *Unforgiveness is like drinking poison yourself*
> *and waiting for the other person to die.*
> ~ Marianne Williamson

You put yourself in your own prison by not forgiving others. You will feel peace and freedom – and healing from the wounds left by anger – in forgiveness.

CRYING

verb – the shedding of tears (or welling of tears in the eyes) in response to an emotional state, pain or a physical irritation of the eye. Emotions that can lead to crying include anger, happiness, or sadness. (Wikipedia)

Crying releases stress. Crying expresses feelings when no words seem suitable. Crying works out anger, depression, and mental fatigue. Crying is a part of the mourning process.

Not everyone cries, and that is okay. We all grieve differently. Try not to judge others for crying when you think they shouldn't, or not crying when you think they should. And don't judge yourself or question yourself if you cry a lot or don't cry at all. We each have our own journey.

It's okay to cry! Let it out!

Sometimes we are in places where we do not feel that it is okay to cry, and we hold it in. We don't want people to ask us why we are crying. We don't want to have to explain to someone, sometimes a total stranger, why we are crying. You may be in line at Walmart and see your loved one's favorite candy bar, and then you start crying. It is okay. Holding it in will wear you out even further.

There may be times when we cry and can't explain why if asked. Crying becomes such a natural part of our days. It seems second nature, and we are not even surprised by our own tears. You may be driving down the road and hear a song on the radio, and the song triggers a memory – and the tears start rolling.

I learned a physically painful lesson during my days of heavy crying. My advice to you: when you are crying, do not wipe your nose and then your eyes with the same tissue. I got a horrible infection, and only a steroid shot in the eyelid could relieve the pain, swelling, and redness.

The man was right who said that salt water was a cure for
everything . . . in one of three forms, tears, sweat, or the sea.
~ Arthur Gordon, *Through Many Windows*

The crying episodes do change over time. They decrease. They are not as deep.

Sad tears can turn into happy tears as we heal. You may actually have tears of joy during your journey. You will experience joy as you recall happy memories, or you remember something that your loved one said, or you see a picture where your loved one is smiling. Someone may reach out to you in such a caring manner that you have tears of appreciation. Tears are not always negative.

Revelation 21:4 (ESV – English Standard Version) reveals a beautiful scene in heaven:

"[God] will wipe away every tear from their eyes."

He wipes away the tears from our loved one who was in so much pain for so long. He wipes away our tears as we go through this grief. He cried with our loved ones as they were in their pain, and He cries with us as we hurt now.

Jesus cried. Go read the passage surrounding that famous Bible verse John 11:35:

Jesus wept.

I find peace in this verse.

And, at the cross, Jesus cried again:

In the days of his flesh,
Jesus offered up prayers and supplications,
with loud cries and tears,
to him who was able to save him from death,
and he was heard because of his reverence.
~ Hebrews 5:7 (ESV)

Even our Jesus, as He walked on this earth, cried. If He did it, so can we.

HOMEWORK

1 – What has denial looked like for you? Do you still find that there are things you are in denial about?

2 – Who are you angry with? Write a letter to each person you feel anger towards. Then burn or shred the letters. Take deep breaths and pray while destroying the letters. Ask God to diffuse your anger.

3 – Have you expressed anger? In what ways, and to whom?

4 – Make the effort to go to those you have expressed anger towards. If you can't go to them face to face, write them a letter. Besides discussing your anger with them or towards them, an apology may be in order. Seek forgiveness.

5 – Do you find yourself crying more now? How does crying make you feel? Have you felt like you shouldn't cry in public or in front of family and friends? Why or why not?

Practical Encouragement

Doing some type of exercise – walking, swimming, riding a bike, or whatever you enjoy – can help reduce anger. Journaling always helps in getting your emotions out/expressed. Also, talking is a healer. Find a friend to listen.

WEEK 4

Fear
Anxiety
Silence

Fear and anxiety are felt early on in this grief. They seem to go hand and hand. It feels like fear and anxiety bring on silence in our lives. The silence will follow you through this entire grief journey.

FEAR

noun – an unpleasant emotion caused by the threat of danger, pain, or harm; a feeling of anxiety concerning the outcome of something or the safety of someone; a mixed feeling of dread and reverence; the likelihood of something unwelcome happening (Lexico.com)

verb – be afraid of (someone or something) as likely to be dangerous, painful, or threatening; feel anxiety on behalf of, avoid doing something because one is afraid (Lexico.com)

Anxiety and terror start long before the loved one dies by suicide. You may have lived with the attempts of suicide. You may have worried that the next attempt would be successful. Your loved one may have expressed threats of the suicide act previously. Your loved one may have had an addiction that led to rehabilitation centers, jail, and broken relationships. There may have been overdoses that your loved one survived. The actual suicide may feel like a relief.

No one ever told me that grief felt so like fear.
~ C.S. Lewis, in the opening line of *A Grief Observed*

The LORD is my light and my salvation—whom shall I fear?
The LORD is the stronghold of my life—of whom
shall I be afraid?
~ Psalm 27:1

Fear comes in the unanswered questions and the unknowns that we experience as soon as our loved one dies by suicide. It's during the process of getting these answers or trying to get these answers that the fear is ever so present. We seem to feel a fear at every turn after our loved one has died by suicide. We feel vulnerable and alone in our fears. The fears can be so overwhelming that we can't even breathe or take our next step. Fear can be paralyzing – mentally, emotionally, and physically.

The following are some of the fears that you may have experienced or may experience in the future:

Will another person in my life abandon me?
Will I want to kill myself?
Will I ever feel safe again?
Will my friends and family disappear?
Can I ever get back to normal again?
Where will I get finances to live?
What happens now?
Was there a life insurance policy – did it pay out, even though the death was by suicide?
Who will do the duties of my loved one?
Who will help me pay the bills?
Will I have to move?
Who am I, now that my loved one is gone?
Who am I now?
How will I pay for the funeral?
Will I get taken advantage of?
Who will cut the grass and take care of household problems?
Who will take care of the children?
Who will wash the clothes and do the shopping?
What will life be like without my loved one?

Some other fears may include:

fear of tomorrow
fear of creating a new normal
fear of moving forward
fear of the unknown

What fears have you experienced that are different from what is listed?

I have learned that, in time, the fears disappear. We start getting the answers to our questions, or we realize that what we had felt in our fear was just NOT reality. A common acronym for FEAR is *False Evidence Appearing Real*. For me, in time, I realized that the meaning of FEAR is *Face Everything And Rise*.

Giving this grief time to run its course is very challenging, especially for those of us who have a hard time being patient or waiting on God's perfect timing. All I can tell you is that the fears will decrease in time. Time is defined differently for each of us. It could be three weeks, six months, a year, or many years. This time of fear is a great time to draw close to God, lean into Him, and give it all to Him. Surrender your fear to Him.

I visualize that I am putting my fears into a box. I put the lid on that box, and then I hand it off to God. When I am handing it off to Him, I am handing it off towards the sky, above my head, as God is the head and the one above me. It is almost humbling for me to hand it off to Him in this fashion. I cannot handle it or be in control. I must let it go. But He can handle these fears of mine, as He is the Great I Am.

> *God said to Moses, "I AM WHO I AM.*
> *This is what you are to say to the Israelites:*
> *'I AM has sent me to you.'"*
> ~ Exodus 3:14

49

In time you realize: life does go on, life is good, life can be rich in love, the sun does shine again, and it all works out. We put one foot in front of the other. Keep Pushing Through. Breathe. Keep trusting God with your journey.

ANXIETY

noun – apprehensive uneasiness or nervousness usually over an impending or anticipated ill; a state of being anxious; mentally distressing concern or interest; a strong desire sometimes mixed with doubt, fear, or uneasiness (Merriam-Webster Dictionary)

Lexico.com defines "anxiety" as *"a nervous disorder characterized by a state of excessive uneasiness and apprehension, typically with a compulsive behavior or panic attacks."* The common physical symptoms of a panic attack associated with anxiety include *"increased heart rate, shortness of breath, muscle tension, sweating, and shaking"* – and it feels scary. Anxiety disorders can have other symptoms such as *"difficulty concentrating, restlessness, irritability, fatigue, insomnia, paranoia, and social withdrawal"* (Myteam.org).

Anxiety in suicide loss grief may be experienced due to trying to avoid any unpleasant thoughts, memories, or emotions about our loved one. Anxiety may come from the feeling that you do not know how to cope with your suicide grief. Whoever plans on having this type of grief in their life? There may be anxiety because those around you are not grieving the same way you are. You are not comfortable with your expression of grief.

Anxiety feels awful. It's frightening and intense. You may feel like you are dying. In your anxiety, you may experience anxiety attacks or panic attacks. Panic attacks create breathing problems and sleep disturbances, and you feel vulnerable. A panic attack or anxiety attack is not controllable by you. This is a physiological response to stress and trauma on the body, either physically or mentally.

I have experienced both. After my brother passed away from a long battle with a brain tumor, I experienced my first full-blown panic attack. I was about to go to bed one night, like any other night. Nothing out of the ordinary had happened this day or night. All of a sudden, my breathing was shallow and rapid, my heart felt like it was beating out of my chest, and I felt like I was suffocating. My blood pressure had also dropped. An ambulance was called, as I felt I was about to die. Internally I kept saying to myself, *"Oh, this is what it feels like to die."*

I didn't die. Eventually, I calmed down and was able to come to a place of rest. I had never had this happen before. I had a panic/anxiety attack. The grief of my brother had caught up with me. I have had other experiences where I was uneasy and facing a situation that created some anxiety in me. I couldn't relax or calm down, and my heart was racing. I had to see a medical doctor as the anxiety attacks became more present in my life.

There isn't a particular event that triggers the attacks. It just happens. I try to practice breathing exercises and to remove myself from the situation I am in when an attack is coming on. Sometimes, medication is necessary. You must do what is best for you in managing your panic or anxiety attacks.

Triggers can increase anxiety during our grief journey. For example, the phone ringing late at night – as that is how and when you were notified that your mother died – may trigger anxiety for you. Or you were notified by the local law enforcement of your loved one's death, so when you see the local law enforcement car come down your street, you experience some panic and your heart starts racing. Or you hear someone say the words *"she committed suicide"*, and it takes you right back to that moment when your loved one died. We can try to control some of the known triggers, but we have no control over external triggers created innocently by others or that are situational.

I have a fear that seems to grow in time. I fear I will forget my boyfriend. You may fear that you will forget your loved one too. We fear that we may forget the memories, the love shared, their laugh, how they smelled, how they looked, their voice, how their hugs felt, how we felt in their presence, just EVERYTHING about them! I do not want to forget his laugh, the way he hugged me, and the way his beard felt when we kissed.

I cherish what I have from my boyfriend: the framed poem he gave me for Christmas and a shirt he sent me in the mail. I have not deleted his voicemails. I still have his texts on my phone. I still have his/our pictures on my phone. I don't ever want to forget him. Do you go back and read the texts from your loved one? Do you go look at the pictures of your loved one?

There was a time when it was bittersweet, but as time has passed, I now have joy looking at his emails, texts, and pictures. I recently went back and read the emails we exchanged when we were first getting to know each other. I smiled the entire time I was reading them. It made my heart happy to read the words we exchanged. I surprised myself because I didn't cry. Healing!

The love we shared will never be forgotten. He will never be forgotten. He will always be a part of my heart – just like your loved one will always be a part of you. We must make sure we put in the effort that will keep our loved ones alive in our hearts and memories. Do it the way that works for you. Try not to let others discourage you from doing what you want to keep your loved one alive in your life.

In this grief, you feel you can't trust the world or the people in it to treat you fairly, which creates anxiety. Always feeling like you are surrounded by others that you can't trust makes you question everyone and everything – which creates anxiety.

Worry never robs tomorrow of its sorrow,
it only saps today of its joy.
~ Leo Buscaglia

Your mind is your prison when you focus on your fear.
~ Tim Fargo

In this suicide loss grief, your personality may change – specifically, the way you look at life. You may feel like disaster can happen at any moment, and you may start focusing on the likelihood of bad things happening.

"If you take that vacation, your plane may crash."

You may believe that the consequences of a proposed event will be worse than they probably will be, and therefore, you experience anxiety before the event. You may avoid the event altogether so as not to have the perceived consequences.

"I don't want to go to church today because I know everyone is going to be looking at me, like I caused it, and they will pass judgment about my son's suicide. So, I am not going to go."

You may be paralyzed by the uncertainty of a bad event taking place, even if the chance of that event taking place is ZERO.

"What if I go shopping today and I am mugged outside the mall?"

Do not be anxious about anything,
but in every situation, by prayer and petition, with thanksgiving,
present your requests to God.
~ Philippians 4:6

Having your personality change can create some anxiety for you. I had a hard time accepting that I wasn't the same person I was before my boyfriend's suicide. This unknown about myself created a new panic for me: *Who am I?*

To get back on track, try going back to the basics of your life: solid sleeping, eating well, exercising, getting back to work, engaging in a social life, and doing activities you enjoy. Seek help from a medical doctor and/or a counselor if the anxiety is unbearable or if panic attacks are present and ongoing.

SILENCE

noun – complete absence of sound or noise; forbearance from speech or noise (Merriam-Webster Dictionary)

verb – to stop someone or something from speaking or making a sound; to prevent someone from giving an opinion or from criticizing you (Macmillan Dictionary)

It seems like silence surrounds a person going through grief from suicide loss. I see silence as the enemy. Silence turns into alienation. Alienation is lonely. Suffering through suicide loss grief alone is hell on earth. The effects of suicide owe their power to silence.

Maybe you have thought that if you remain silent and do not speak of the truth of suicide, then maybe it will not really be suicide. But this isn't rational thinking.

Silence will not cure a disease.
On the contrary, it will make it worse.
~ Leo Tolstoy

People do not want to talk about events surrounding a suicide. Most people do not even want to admit it was a death by suicide.

"Do we have to tell the family how he died?"
"Just tell people that he was sold a drug and it was laced with something that killed him."
"If anyone asks you how your uncle died, just act like you don't hear them."
"If we don't have a funeral or memorial service, we don't have to answer the questions of how she died."

It may not be us who are silent, but others. Others may shy away from us or avoid us because they do not know what to say. They stay silent towards us. I have tried not to be upset or hurt when others are silent towards me. People are awkward and just do not know what to say to us – but, most of the time, we just want to know people are there for us. They don't need to have particular words for us. They just need to be present.

With a suicide, silence is an attempt to keep a lid on terrible accusations toward others and oneself. Family members/friends don't want to expose blame and guilt by blaming other family members/friends, and they don't want to experience the guilt themselves. Even if family members feel that the suicide was someone's fault (blame) or that the death was their own fault (self-blame), it will not be verbally expressed. Everyone stays quiet. People think that if they don't have to talk about it, they don't have to deal with the "fault" of the suicide. If you don't talk about it, maybe it won't be true – maybe it wasn't really suicide.

The protective mask for people suffering through suicide grief is silence, but silence leads to inability to lead a productive life. Silence keeps a person in bondage. We do not have control over others, but we do have control over ourselves. We can talk, share and be open about what we have experienced, what our loved one was going through, and our expectations.

55

"Can you please sit with me and listen while I talk about my mom?"

"Do you mind sitting with me while I talk about my son's last conversation with me?"

"Let me share what I know about my daughter's death by suicide."

There is healing in talking. End the silence about your loved one's suicide. Discussion is natural and beneficial, as it allows for expression of pain, sorrow, anger, and frustration. Even though society has made us feel shame, there is no shame that our loved one died by suicide. There is no shame in the method of death.

Our loved one's suicide does not define their character. Suicide does not mean a person is "bad" or that they are burning in hell. Suicide is a method of death, like cancer or a car accident. As much as society wants to cast shame, guilt, or blame on suicide – as much as they want to be silent about it – we do not have to follow that same path.

Now, there is a time for silence. That is when we need to be listening to God. Not all times of silence are negative or in need of ending. It is healing to be in silence and to meditate. It is when we are not discussing or avoiding the fact that our loved one died by suicide that silence is not healthy.

Open up and talk. Also know when to listen.

Be still, and know that I am God . . .
~ Psalm 46:10a (KJV – King James Version)

HOMEWORK

1 – What do you fear the most? Why?

2 – Look at the list of fears in this chapter. Which have you experienced? Have you experienced any not listed? Journal about them.

3 – What types of anxiety have you experienced? What ways do you cope with your anxiety? What have you done to reduce or eliminate anxiety from your life?

4 – How has silence affected you? How does it make you feel?

5 – Think of a couple things that you are fearful to do. Pray about those things, ask God for strength, then go do the thing that you feel God gives you the strength to go do.

Practical Encouragement

Be silent in a positive way. Go for a walk. Meditate. Do yoga. Journal. Pray. Enjoy your hobby in silence. Go for a walk out in nature and listen to the birds. Listen in your silence.

WEEK 5

Guilt
Shame
Notes

The grief in suicide loss is wrapped up in guilt and shame. The shame in suicide loss grief is complicated. Shame and guilt on the suicide loss journey look very different from grief caused by other kinds of death. How do we process guilt and shame in our grief? We will discuss that in this chapter. We will also discuss the infamous notes left – or not left – by our loved one.

GUILT

noun – the fact of having committed a breach of conduct, especially violating law and involving a penalty (Merriam-Webster Dictionary); the state of one who has committed an offense, especially consciously; feelings of deserving blame, especially for imagined offenses or from a sense of inadequacy (Betterhelp.com); deserving blame or censure as being wrong or evil or injurious (Reversedictionary.org)

verb – to cause (someone) to feel guilty; to persuade (someone) to do something by causing feelings of guilt (Merriam-Webster Dictionary)

"Come, let us return to the LORD.
He has torn us to pieces
but He will heal us;
He has injured us
but He will bind up our wounds.

After two days He will revive us;
on the third day He will restore us,
that we may live in His presence.
Let us acknowledge the LORD;
let us press on to acknowledge Him.
As surely as the sun rises,
He will appear;
He will come to us like the winter rains,
like the spring rains that water the earth."
~ Hosea 6:1-3

As far as the east is from the west,
so far has he removed our transgressions from us.
~ Psalm 103:12

Guilt is in the statements of *"If only", "I should have", "I could have", "What if", "Why didn't I".* We can't change the past, so we need to try not to dwell on these statements. These types of statements can totally consume our lives. They will hinder our healing process. We need to try to let go of these statements and Push Through.

There is guilt both before and after the death. You may feel guilty that you didn't give the addict daughter money to go get drugs so she could satisfy her addiction. Or you feel you have failed in raising your children due to their not-so-acceptable and disappointing behaviors/decisions as adults. Or you have guilt because you feel you didn't do all you could have done to save your marriage. You have a sense of helplessness built into the guilt: *"I had no more inside of me to give; it's my fault."* You may even feel the guilt of *"You did this to me"* from your loved one – which seems to be coming from the grave.

Most people who have lost someone to suicide feel guilt for not seeing the signs, for not taking their loved one seriously, for not listening, for not doing something for the loved one, and for feeling like they failed their loved one. Our guilt carries so many different kinds of guilty feelings with it that we are also confused.

You may need to feel guilty for a little while to process through it. Guilt is a natural emotion after a death. Eventually, you come to accept that you are not responsible for the death of your loved one. You had no control over their decision. There is nothing you could have done. Prayerfully, you will be able to Push Through the prior-to-death guilt feelings as well.

There is such a thing as good guilt. Good guilt comes from God when we have sinned, and it leads to repentance and forgiveness. This is appropriate and real. It has a place in our lives. But good guilt does not exist in suicide loss grief.

There is also bad guilt. Bad guilt comes from unreasonable expectations – either our own or others'. Bad guilt is not from God.

Have you heard the term "Suicide Survivor"? It applies to a person who has lost someone to suicide and who is surviving the aftermath of that loss. I do not like this term, as it seems confusing to me. People who hear it could think it refers to someone who attempted suicide and was not successful. I prefer "Suicide Loss Survivor" instead.

Speaking of being a survivor: there is such a thing as survivor's guilt. As Wikipedia defines it, *"Survivor guilt is a mental condition that occurs when a person believes they have done something wrong by surviving a traumatic event when others did not, often feeling self-guilt."* We will all experience some level of this survivor's guilt. It is normal to feel survivor's guilt, and it can be experienced in all types of death, not just in suicide loss.

Survivor's guilt is bad guilt if it remains in our journey longer than it should. If you are experiencing survivor's guilt, you may want to ask for forgiveness from your loved one through God. You should also ask God for a change in your perspective concerning what you feel in your guilt.

"Lord, I am feeling guilty for not taking my son to rehab. Please forgive me. I ask for forgiveness through you, Lord, since I cannot ask my son for that forgiveness."

Remorse/regret is feeling bad about what you did: *"I feel horrible that I yelled at her the night before she took her life."* Guilt is feeling bad about who you are: *"I am such a fat slob."* Regret has a purpose, telling you something that needs to be fixed. Guilt, on the other hand, just pulls you down. Guilt can paralyze you if you let it.

Guilt affects our reasoning: *"I should have listened when he told me he was going to 'eat a bullet.' I didn't listen. I didn't take him seriously. I am a bad person."* Just as the suicide was irrational, so is guilt in suicide loss grief. Guilt is irrational and keeps you from functioning at 100%. It saps energy from you – but only if you let it. For us in this journey, guilt will be a downer for us. It will keep us from moving forward in our journey. Try to let it go and Push Through!!!

You may have been able to delay the suicide, but when a person is determined that life is unbearable, they will end it regardless of any intervention efforts. I found out after my boyfriend's death that he had tried at least four times to take his life, starting in 2006, ten years prior to his death. I had one of his prior co-workers tell me about his two or three attempts while on active duty military. I also saw printed materials indicating two suicidal occasions in Iraq, after his military service was over and he was working as a contractor.

My boyfriend texted me two times during drinking binges that he *"would eat a bullet."* I did not take him seriously. He was very drunk, so I did not think he would actually take his own life. But, could I really have changed the outcome, or just delayed it again for him?! No, I couldn't have changed the outcome. He had been in pain for over ten years, if not more. My heart aches for him and the pain he endured in silence for so many years.

Because of all I discovered early on in my grief journey about my boyfriend – his pain, his life, his past, and his present – I made a huge effort to let go of the guilt. It was not my choice that he died by suicide. It was his choice alone.

"He will wipe every tear from their eyes.
There will be no more death' or mourning or crying or pain,
for the old order of things has passed away."
~ Revelation 21:4

For God did not send his Son into the world
to condemn the world,
but to save the world through him.
~ John 3:17

None of us are so powerful that we have control over someone else. We could not have stopped the suicide. People make their own choices. We have freewill. Your loved one had freewill. We cannot govern anyone 24/7 or control everything that happens in someone's life. We cannot even control everything in our own lives, much less someone else's.

It was not our fault. We could not have stopped the suicide. We must accept that it was our loved one's choice to end their life. All we can do is disagree with the decision. The choice they made is out of our control.

The LORD is compassionate and gracious,
slow to anger, abounding in love.
He will not always accuse,
nor will He harbor His anger forever;
He does not treat us as our sins deserve
or repay us according to our iniquities.
For as high as the heavens are above the earth,
so great is His love for those who fear Him;
as far as the east is from the west,
so far has he removed our transgressions from us.
~ Psalm 103:8-12

SHAME

noun – a painful feeling of humiliation or distress caused by the consciousness of wrong or foolish behavior (Lexico.com)

verb – to make someone feel nervous, ashamed, or stupid in a social situation (Macmillan Dictionary)

In suicide loss grief, we tend to judge ourselves harshly, which leads to shame. We are too critical of ourselves. We feel complete disgust, revulsion, contemptibility, disgrace, dishonor, and condemnation toward ourselves in our grief process. Not only do we feel these things towards ourselves, but we feel like others outside of the suicide loss grief circle feel the same way towards us. Shame is so confusing. And messy.

Some people also experience shame about the fact that their loved one died by suicide. There shouldn't be judgment about someone's method of death, but in suicide, it seems to be present – which creates more confusion for us about our own feelings of shame. Listen to me: there is no shame that our loved one died by suicide. We should not carry the perceived shame on behalf of our loved one. Their method of death does not indicate that our loved one was a bad person or of bad character.

Shame is a learned response, like fear. Others shame us. In shame, we do not want to share our story due to the death being suicide. We will feel judged: *"Did you not know your loved one was depressed or that they wanted to end their life?"* When people ask questions like that, we hear: *"Why didn't you stop them from taking their life?"* *"Seriously, I would have died so he could have lived."* When we feel judged by others, we will also think there is a need to feel shame.

Shame says, *"I am a bad person."* Shame indicates that I failed to do my part. A shame statement is *"If I had . . ."* We cannot change the past. We can only move forward and learn from the past. We must continue to Push Through.

You did nothing wrong in your loved one's dying by suicide. You are not a bad person. I had no part in my boyfriend's death. You are not responsible for your loved one's death. Our role in our loved one's life was not a failure. We must accept that we have no control over another person's decisions – in how they are living their life, or if they end their life.

The less we talk about or share our shame experiences with others, the more power shame has in our lives. Talk to someone you trust. Their empathy will help in dissolving the shame feelings you carry. Remember: living in shame is not productive or healthy.

Our journey out of this confusing grief can bring unexpected good. We may learn that we were living unconsciously until the suicide, taking life for granted. In a positive way, the suicide awakens us to live in the now. Now we can live with awareness and gratitude, leaving any shame in the past.

What can we do with this shame.? How do we deal with it? We talk, we share, we reach out to others, and we take positive actions. According to *Psychology Today*, there are five ways to end shame.

1- *Bring shame into light*
2- *Untangle what you feel*
3- *Unhitch what you do from who you are*
4- *Recognize your triggers*
5- *Make connections*

NOTES

Was there a note or some other communication from your loved one that was left behind or discovered? Only a small percentage of notes are left/found. *"It is estimated that 25–30% of suicides are accompanied by a note"* (Wikipedia.org). I believe we all want answers, or at least to see into the world of our loved one at the time when they decided to end their life. We think a note will give us those answers.

Do we want to know they loved us? Do we want to know what was wrong? Do we want to know what they were feeling? Do we want to know who they blamed? Do we want to know what their wishes were after their death? Do we want to know what motivated them to end their life? Do we want to understand why they felt they were a burden?

Even if a note was left, the note (handwritten, email, text message) does not tell the whole story of our loved one. The note will not include the chemical imbalances of our loved one or their inability to function rationally. (Often, mental illness is coupled with alcohol or substance abuse when a suicide takes place.) The note may contain a to-do list, harsh words to someone left behind, an apology, or a partial explanation about the mystery of their death. Or it may not make any sense at all.

I recommend not putting too much weight into what was written in a note. It may add to the pain more than lessen it.

The painful questions won't get answers in a note left behind. The note may even lead to more questions. Our loved one was not rational when they took their life. Even if the note seems to make some sense, remember: our loved one's issues were very deep. If they had been able to fully articulate their pain, maybe they would not have been so desperate to end their life.

Not all notes left are pleasant. Some are filled with depressive, guilty, shameful, hurtful, and angry sentiments. None of those are what we want to hear. Such words could create even more guilt and anger towards the deceased, ourselves, or others. The anger would be defensive, as there is no way to defend from the attack written in the note. You may feel guilty because of the loved one pointing out that there was something you did or did not do. Or their written perception was nowhere close to what reality was. The note could contain nothing but lies. Negativity in notes brings even more pain to those left behind.

What if the words in the note are true? What if the deceased spouse states in their note that their spouse committed infidelity, and it is true? There is a difference between guilt for the action and guilt for your loved one's suicide. Forgive yourself if there truly was wrong on your part. Still, remember: one person, one emotion, or one event is not responsible for a suicide. Suicide is the result of a perfect storm consisting of a mixture of any of the following: mental illness, addiction, societal hurts, failed coping skills, hopelessness, emotional pain, genetic influences, distorted thoughts, and physical pain.

Does the note really offer any comfort, or does it make the grief process worse? Would it help you to keep going back to look at that note, which stirs up negative emotions and thoughts? Or would you rather look at happy pictures and read happy text messages? Focusing on the positive remembrances will help in healthy healing.

Remember: the feelings in the note represent a moment, not the entire life of the person who takes their life. If a note contains negative words about you, it was a moment of your loved one's life – not the entire life you two had together. The note does not represent your loved one's life, just like suicide does not represent who your loved one was.

Not only so, but we also glory in our sufferings,
because we know that suffering produces perseverance;
perseverance, character; and character, hope.
And hope does not put us to shame,
because God's love has been poured out into our hearts
through the Holy Spirit, who has been given to us.
~ Romans 5:3-5

HOMEWORK

1 – What have you felt guilt over? Do others make you feel guilty? Write about your guilt experience in your journal.

2 – Are you embarrassed and ashamed about the suicide? How have you expressed it?

3 – Did your loved one leave a note? If so, do you feel it was a true picture of what was really going on with your loved one?

4 – Do you think shame or guilt were being experienced by your loved one? How so? What do you think made your loved one feel guilt or shame?

5 – Are you carrying the burdens of your loved one that do not belong to you? Why? How can this change? How can you turn shame and guilt around to the positive?

Practical Encouragement

Go for a walk or some form of exercise that allows you to think. After it is over, take your journal out and write about whatever thoughts or feelings you had while exercising.

Find a Bible verse that helps you get through these feelings. Write it on a card and paste it on a mirror or your phone or somewhere you will see it often. When the guilt/shame feelings rise up, choose to focus on the words of that verse instead.

WEEK 6

Mourning
Memories
Self-Esteem

We mourn during the grieving process, and we all do it differently after a loss due to suicide. Our self-esteem may suffer in this grief journey. In suicide loss grief, our memories are different than in other types of grief. They are tainted. Yet, we need to learn how to remember our loved one in positive and loving ways.

MOURNING

noun – an expression of grief or a time of grieving that follows a loved one's death or other serious loss (Vocabulary.com)

When they lifted up their eyes at a distance
and did not recognize him, they raised their voices and wept.
And each of them tore his robe
and they threw dust over their heads toward the sky.
Then they sat down on the ground with him
for seven days and seven nights
with no one speaking a word to him,
for they saw that his pain was very great.
~ Job 2:12-13 (NASB – New American Standard Bible)

The word "mourning" is perceived differently by most. Some see it as showing remembrance to someone by a funeral or memorial service, having friends and family into the home for visitation, wearing black clothing, and putting a memorial wreath at the front door. Some see this time as immediately after the death and lasting only a few days. Others may see it as a period that not only happens right after the death, but also at various times during the grief process and into the years beyond. Whatever it is for you is just fine.

During the mourning period, take time to think about your loved one and the relationship you had with them. The mourning process gives us a chance to say or express how we feel about the person who died. We get to shed tears, we express our anger, and we share with others about our loss and the pain of our loved one's departure. Mourning is both private and public. You may express your mourning differently in private than you do in public, and that is ok.

It's almost relieving to know that we only mourn what we love, and that love will never fade in time.

> *How lucky I am to have something*
> *that makes saying goodbye so hard.*
> ~Winnie the Pooh

During the mourning period, people will say things that are inappropriate, rude, stupid, silly, and hurtful.

"You will get over it."
"Why didn't you see the signs and help her?"
"He was just a selfish alcoholic."

Try to listen to their heart; they probably did not mean to cause harm with their words. Here is your chance to show compassion to others. Most people just do not know exactly what to say to ease your pain or to show they care, so they end up saying things they shouldn't. Be compassionate towards them as they do try to put forth the effort.

Do not feel guilty about the way you mourn. It can be different than other family members or friends who have the same loss. That is okay. Don't try to understand why people mourn differently than you. Trying to understand why others are experiencing their grief differently will consume your thoughts. So, just let it go. Do it your way - whatever works best for you. Push Through.

Some people will wear black clothing when they mourn. Some people will meet up with friends to have a toast at a local bar. Some people keep to themselves. Others will want to be around other people to outwardly express their mourning. You may choose to put a flower wreath at the front door indicating a death. You may want to have a party-like atmosphere with friends and family. There seem to be more and more memorials or "celebration of life" types of mourning currently. There may be a funeral or a visitation at the home. Some people will do nothing.

I chose to have a "celebration of life" for my boyfriend by a water fountain that had an angel statue. He loved the water. My boyfriend taught me valuable lessons about being the light, and I chose to share that: I handed out flashlights at his "celebration of life" ceremony. To this day, I sometimes get a random text from a friend or a picture of the flashlight I handed out, with a message that my friend used the flashlight and thought of me and my boyfriend.

Unfortunately, it seems there is division when it comes to death. With families and loved ones not agreeing on funerals, memorial services, or "celebration of life" ceremonies, you may have to do your own type of mourning-expression. It is hurtful when you can't come together at this time, and don't be surprised when everyone doesn't get along. There is a lot of tension because of the conflicted emotions that each person who loved your loved one is carrying.

Mourning can't be rushed. Be patient. There is no timetable that is right or wrong concerning your mourning. The way you mourn may depend on cultural or religious traditions. The way your family does their mourning may also have a huge impact on your mourning process. Mourning will last until you feel at peace over your loss and you accept the suicide. It will take as long as it takes. You get to decide this. No one else gets to decide your mourning time frame or how you mourn. Mourning is as personal as your favorite flavor of ice cream. Be you and Push Through.

Mourning doesn't only happen immediately after the death. It can take place at other times, like an anniversary, birthday, a holiday that was important to your loved one, remembrance of a special time together, or at any triggered moment. It is okay to have different times when you feel you need to mourn your loved one. This is your journey. Mourn when and how you choose.

It is very necessary to mourn – but don't get stuck in the process. Don't stay in it too long, to the point when it is more harmful than helpful in your healing. Push Through. As with any stage of suicide loss grief, if you are struggling at any time, seek professional medical or counseling help.

"Yet even now," declares the LORD, "Turn back to me with your whole heart, with fasting, tears, and mourning."
~ Joel 2:12 (ISV)

MEMORIES

noun – Something remembered from the past (Lexico.com); the mental capacity or faculty of retaining, recalling, and reviving facts, events, impressions, etc. (Dictionary.com)

Memories tend to be tainted when there was a suicide. The unanswered questions that go with our memories seem to diminish what was once a positive recollection of our loved one.

We look at the pictures of our loved one and ask ourselves, *"Was he thinking about ending his life here?"*.

Or we remember a shared moment and ask ourselves, *"Was she happy when we went to the state fair together?"*.

We may recall a time when we thought our loved one was happy and enjoying the moment, then ask ourselves, *"Were they faking their happiness?"*.

Most of the memories are not enjoyable after the death because we question ourselves with each one. More unanswered questions. Our loved one made the choice to end their life, and the pain of their choice taints every happy moment we had. The memory goes from being wonderful to being not so satisfying – almost sad.

If you were the person who found your loved one after the suicide, that memory may be a forefront memory for a very long time. Or the memory of when you got the news and how you felt at that moment may be a forefront memory. And some memories, like the discovery that our loved one died by suicide, are memories we want to forget.

With our strongest and most painful memories of our loved one, we hope to never repeat that exact pain in that moment. I am here to tell you: that intense and life-sucking pain you first felt will never be repeated. The pain will come close, but it won't be as intense. The current or future pain will not be that ugly and breathtaking moment when you found your loved one or found out that your loved one died by suicide.

Think about the sport of bungee jumping. When a person takes that leap off the bridge, they plunge down to the end point where they almost touch the water. Then they spring back up towards the bridge, then plunge down towards the water – but they don't go as far down the second or third or fourth time, because the momentum of the bungee band is decreasing. The pain associated with the memory of discovery about our loved one is just like this. The intensity decreases. Just like the overall pain of our loss, the pain of the memories loses momentum over time.

We may forget the bad memories and then only remember the good ones. It is a natural defense to push the bad memories out of our minds. The experience of our loved one's suicide is bad enough without having to rehash the bad memories we had with them before their death. It is normal to want to cling to the good memories.

Over time, as we cling to the good times and enjoyable memories, we may forget that our loved one caused us much pain by their addiction or any behavior that was negative, abusive, or hurtful. In suicide loss grief – when there were no goodbyes, and no chance to make wrongs right – we are more apt to keep the fond memories closer. And that is a good thing.

Or, since it was a suicide, we may get focused on the negative memories instead of the good ones. We may even flip-flop between the good and bad memories. Bad memories may be about the struggles that our loved one had – struggles with alcohol or drug addiction, the torments of mental illness, or the relationship battles. These memories may override any good times. And it seems these bad memories are prevalent just because our loved one died by suicide. Since suicide is a personal choice, we focus on the negative – of the person, of the past, and of our memories with them.

When we find ourselves focusing on the negative memories, we may want to journal, talk with a professional, chat with a friend, go for a walk, practice relaxation techniques, or go do an activity that gets our mind off of our present thinking pattern. It is during this negative time that a gratitude journal may come in handy.

I am sure you will spend time focusing on both the good and the bad memories. It is normal, and you shouldn't feel guilty for any of it. Don't feel guilty for experiencing the bad memories, but don't let them keep you from clinging to your good ones. Go with it! Push Through!

There are so many ways to keep the memory of your loved one alive. It's entirely dependent on how you want to do it, but here are some ideas to get you going:

~ *Create a scrapbook full of pictures, handwritten notes, or any memorabilia of your loved one*
~ *Commit random acts of kindness*
~ *Plant a flower, plant, tree, or bush*
~ *Get a special pendant or piece of jewelry made*
~ *Paint a picture or sculpt a piece of pottery*
~ *Write a story about your loved one*
~ *Make a keepsake box full of memorabilia*
~ *Create a website or use social media as the outlet*
~ *Start a blog*
~ *Wear a piece of clothing that belonged to your loved one*
~ *Enjoy an event that was enjoyed together in the past (sporting event, social event, a vacation, a special place visited, etc.)*
~ *Make a home video of pictures*
~ *Create a scholarship fund*
~ *Get a tattoo*
~ *Have others write down their memories of your loved one*
~ *Start a grief support group for others who have lost someone to suicide or overdose*

The possibilities are endless as to how you want to preserve the memories of your loved one. You may want to do this as a family, with friends of your loved one, or alone. Whatever brings you peace and makes you happy is how you should keep your memories alive.

There is one thing that no one can take from us, and it is our memories. As in all aspects of life, focus on the good. Keep your good memories close, and try not to let any bad memories shadow the happiness that the good memories bring to your soul.

SELF-ESTEEM

noun – confidence in one's own worth or abilities; self-respect (Lexico.com)

"Low self-esteem is characterized by a lack of confidence and feeling badly about oneself. People with low self-esteem often feel unlovable, awkward, or incompetent." (Psychalive.com) When a person has low self-esteem, negative thoughts are present. *"Negative thoughts bring about negative self-criticism. With self-criticism, there can be feelings of sadness, depression, anxiety, anger, shame, or guilt."* (Betterhealth.vic.gov.au)

We already know that these feelings of sadness, depression, anxiety, anger, shame, and guilt are present in suicide loss grief. It is understandable for us to suffer from low self-esteem due to our feet being knocked out from under us by this experience of loss. I was shocked at how deeply I suffered from low self-esteem. The low self-esteem created more loneliness for me. Who wants to be around others when they have low self-esteem? Isolation is a by-product of low self-esteem.

Our life is shattered. Not only is our loved one gone, but we don't know why – and we never will. Our new normal is unknown and uncomfortable. We have secondary wounds that may never heal. The relationships that once were our anchor are now wavering. We feel like a failure. We feel incomplete without our loved one. The low self-esteem will follow us into our other relationships. It may come into our workplace, our romantic relationship, or into any area where we are in a leadership position – being the boss at work, as a community leader, or in parenting.

The following are possible thoughts you may feel or have felt in this grief journey:

"What did I do wrong for my daughter to end her life?"
"Will my other children want to take their life? I feel like a failed parent."
"I am no good – my husband left me."
"I was such a disappointment to my mother that she took her life."
"No one loves me."
"It should have been me that died, not my sister. I was the screwed-up kid in the family."

You have what it takes. You can do this. You can get through this grief process. Push Through.

I can do all this through him who gives me strength.
~ Philippians 4:13

We may have seen low self-esteem in our loved one who died by suicide. Then we realize we are in a similar place in our grief journey, and this may make us feel that we also want to die by suicide. Don't panic: it is normal to experience low self-esteem in this journey of grief. Get into counseling if your low self-esteem lasts longer than you – or trusted friends around you – think it should. Only you can determine how long you can handle what you are faced with in this grief. Counseling is an excellent place to sort out your feelings.

There are ways to improve your self-esteem. Pursue relationships by surrounding yourself with those who lift you up and encourage you. To help in ceasing the self-criticisms, make a list of self-affirmations. Replace negative thoughts with positive thoughts. Forgive yourself, your loved one who died by suicide, and others. Love others and treat them as you would like to be treated. Get out there and exercise.

Your circumstances do not define you. But your efforts in Pushing Through will define you.

Thinking, deciding, and acting should not be based on emotions. Make decisions based on what is best for you. Be you! Express to others verbally what you need, want, like, don't like, and don't want, and be true to yourself during this time of grief. Be good to yourself; no one is perfect.

Forgive yourself. Respect yourself. Love yourself! Then you can forgive others, respect others, and love others!

You are worth it!

Let us then approach God's throne of grace with confidence,
so that we may receive mercy and find grace to help us
in our time of need.
~ Hebrews 4:16

HOMEWORK

1 – How have you mourned your loved one? Did you have a funeral, memorial service, "celebration of life," or no formal gathering? What led to the decision of this type of mourning for you and your family?

2 – When do you feel like you have mourned? Was it immediately after the death of your loved one, or at other times? How do you continue to outwardly mourn your loved one?

3 – Journal about your favorite memories with your loved one, things you want to remember about your loved one, and the lessons you learned from your loved one. Decide how you are going to preserve the memories; you can choose from the list above, or you can invent your own way.

4 – If there are memories you would like to forget, write them down and then burn them. Ask God to remove these memories from your mind.

5 – Do you feel you have low self-esteem because of this grief? Did your loved one have low self-esteem or other self-worth issues? Write yourself a letter. Write about all of your good qualities, your purpose, good memories with your loved one, and times in life that have made you laugh.

Practical Encouragement

This week, do yoga or go for a walk, a run, a swim, or a bike ride. Get moving. Increasing your heart rate will increase the good feelings in your body and soul.

WEEK 7

Crisis of Faith
Trusting God

Have you wondered where God is in all of this? In suicide, in death, in grief, in your life, in your loved one's life, in the world? This grief may even have you wondering if God exists. And if He does, how could He do this to you? How could He let your loved one die by suicide?

The secret things belong to the LORD our God,
but the things revealed belong to us
and to our children forever,
that we may follow all the words of this law.
~ Deuteronomy 29:29

CRISIS OF FAITH

It seems that blaming God was the first place I went. Not blaming my boyfriend. Not blaming the alcohol he had been drinking for seven days straight. Not blaming the PTSD. I blamed GOD! If God loved me and my boyfriend, why did God let this happen?

Where is God in suicide? Why did God let this happen to my loved one? Is this what God wanted? Did God cause this? Where is God in ALL of this? Why, God? Where are You? Why would God do this to me? What did I do to deserve this pain? Why did God do this to my loved one? Why didn't God stop my loved one from taking their life? Where is God in this awkward grief journey?

You have searched me, LORD, and you know me.
You know when I sit and when I rise;
you perceive my thoughts from afar.
You discern my going out and my lying down;
you are familiar with all my ways.
Before a word is on my tongue you, LORD, know it completely.
You hem me in behind and before,
and you lay your hand upon me.
~ Psalm 139:1-5

Psalm 139 is my answer for my God-questions. He knows everything – not just about me, but about you, and about our loved one who died by suicide.

My frame was not hidden from you
when I was made in the secret place,
when I was woven together in the depths of the earth.
Your eyes saw my unformed body;
all the days ordained for me were written in your book
before one of them came to be.
~ Psalm 139:15-16

This verse gives me so much peace about my boyfriend's life. God loved my boyfriend before my boyfriend was even created in his mother's womb. God loves my boyfriend more than my boyfriend's parents could love him – more than his siblings, family, friends, or even I, the girlfriend, could. My boyfriend's pains on this earth made God sad. But God knew all about those pains and hurts. God loved him anyway – just as He loves us anyway.

I am so thankful that God doesn't love me BECAUSE _____ (fill in the blank with a reason). He just loves us. Period.

This verse also reminded me that my days are ordained by God, just as my boyfriend's days were ordained by God. God did not cause my boyfriend to die by suicide, but He knew it was going to happen. I do struggle thinking that God had this knowledge – that my boyfriend would die that way, by suicide, and that all who loved my boyfriend would hurt the way that we do. But, in time, I was able to take comfort in this: God was not surprised by my boyfriend's death or by my pain. He did not abandon my boyfriend, and He will not abandon me.

I could not change the way my boyfriend's life ended, but I could choose to continue trusting in the goodness and power of God. It took me a while to come to this place of acceptance, but I did come to it. It took me a while to trust God with my pain. But, by Pushing Through, I was able to trust again.

I have a vision: my boyfriend is on the beach, in such mental pain, about to take his life. God is kneeling beside my boyfriend with His hand on my boyfriend's shoulder. God is weeping; His child is in deep pain. God doesn't want His child to hurt, physically or mentally. God doesn't want my boyfriend to take his life. But my boyfriend has free will. God lets each of us make our own decisions in life. God's will does not override our free will.

Suicide reminds us that we live in a broken world. We have free will in this broken world. God allows us to make choices about our lives through free will. It is with free will that a person chooses to end their life. God doesn't make them do it. God did not take our loved one from us. Our loved one took themselves away from us, their pain, and this life on this earth.

No temptation has overtaken you except what is common to mankind. And God is faithful; he will not let you be tempted beyond what you can bear. But when you are tempted, he will also provide a way out so that you can endure it.
~ 1 Corinthians 10:13

God knows what tempts us. He knows what we feel. God can make a way for us in our pain.

The LORD is good to all; he has compassion on all he has made.
~ Psalm 145:9

God has compassion for all He has made – which means you, me, and our loved one who died by suicide. In this verse, replace the word compassion with "suffer with." He suffers with us and experiences our pain like we do. How awesome it is that God actually knows and suffers with us, as He did with our loved one.

Believe it or not, but the word "suicide" is not a modern word. Suicide is mentioned in the Bible in several places. Does it surprise you that suicide is in the Bible? Please read on your own about these times of suicide in the Bible:

1 – Abimelech (Judges 9:52-55)

2 – Samson (Judges 16:28-30)

3 – Saul (1 Samuel 31:3-6)

4 – Saul's armor bearer (1 Samuel 31:3-6)

5 – Ahithophel (2 Samuel 17:23)

6 – Zimri (1 Kings 16:18-19)

7 – Judas Iscariot (Matthew 27:3-5) – only reference to "suicide" in the New Testament

One question probably goes through everyone's mind, even those outside the familial circle: *"Is my loved one in hell?" "Did my co-worker go to hell?" "Did the lady who sang in the church choir with me go to hell when she took her life?"* If your loved one had a personal relationship with Jesus Christ, then they did not go to hell. But do we really know about that personal relationship – not just with our loved one who died by suicide, but with anyone? No, we do not.

86

We do not know what was between our loved one and God. Our loved one could have screamed out to God in their final moments and asked for forgiveness. We have no idea. We have to trust.

Jesus replied, "Very truly I tell you, no one can see the kingdom of God unless they are born again."
~ John 3:3

If someone dies a more socially accepted method of death like old age, a car accident, or cancer, we don't sit around, pondering and questioning if that person is in hell. Society wants to immediately condemn the act of suicide to hell.

Religions teach their own views on suicide. Some religions state that, if a person takes their own life, they do not go to heaven. This is nowhere in the Bible. This thought comes from man-made religious law.

Becoming a Christian does not stop a person from sinning. "Thou shall not murder" is one of the ten commandments. Therefore, suicide is sin – but a single sin does not take salvation from a person.

Think about this example: Jason is outside in his front yard playing basketball with his son. Jason's neighbor pulls up, driving a brand-new Corvette. Jason is very jealous and envious of his neighbor. Jason yells over to his neighbor, *"Hey Tim, I have always wanted a Corvette. You are one lucky man. I am so jealous."* Not five minutes later, Jason has a massive heart attack in the driveway. We don't know for sure, but Jason probably didn't have time to ask for forgiveness for the sin of jealousy. Does that mean Jason went straight to hell? No.

A lot of people have misconstrued what suicide is or isn't in spiritual/religious practices, and they believe that suicide is the "unforgivable" or "unpardonable" sin. Is suicide an unforgivable sin? No. Is suicide unpardonable? No. The only unforgivable or unpardonable sin is blaspheming the Holy Spirit.

"Truly I tell you, people can be forgiven all their sins
and every slander they utter,
but whoever blasphemes against the Holy Spirit
will never be forgiven; they are guilty of an eternal sin."
~ Mark 3:28-29

People claim that suicide is self-murder. This is true. God knows that the person was in grave distress. God knows His child was not in a good mental state. God wants His children with Him in heaven. God is not going to send His child to hell because of one sin.

Do you not know that your bodies are temples of the Holy Spirit,
who is in you, whom you have received from God?
You are not your own; you were bought at a price.
Therefore, honor God with your bodies.
~ 1 Corinthians 6:19-20

The Bible doesn't state that we will be eternally damned if we die by suicide. Yes, your loved one did not honor their body by self-murder. But the Bible doesn't state that we are eternally damned for dishonoring our body.

What if your loved one had died in a tragic car accident and, right before it happened, they told a lie? Would they go to hell for telling that lie right before death? No. All sins are equal. One sin is not greater than another. The act of suicide does not send a person to hell.

Suicide is an act of desperation – a way to end the pain. What kind of life did that person lead? Was it filled with kindness, love, and selflessness? Suicide is irrational. A single act does not negate a person's entire character and moral identity.

Christians tend to judge and speculate in a situation like suicide, but God is the only righteous judge. God is just and perfect in wisdom. God considers our loved one's mind. The mind is restored as our loved one enters eternity, healed of depression, addiction, or other mental illness.

NOTHING separates God from His children.

For I am convinced that neither death nor life,
neither angels nor demons, neither the present nor the future,
nor any powers, neither height nor depth,
nor anything else in all creation, will be able to separate us from
the love of God that is in Christ Jesus our Lord.
~ Romans 8:38-39

God feels pain as intensely as we do. He wraps His loving arms around His children and tries to comfort them – not only our loved one who took their life, but us too. When we are sad, mad, resistant towards Him, and not able to feel His comfort, He does not throw us away and forget about us – just as He didn't throw away or forget about our loved one.

We trust His love and forgiveness. His love and forgiveness extend to His children who take their lives.

I have no doubt that God grieves with His child as they are in that moment of taking their life. He is right there beside them. Crying. His child is in great agony and no longer wants to be on this earth. It pains God for His children to be in pain.

Praise be to the God and Father of our Lord Jesus Christ,
the Father of compassion and the God of all comfort,
who comforts us in all our troubles,
so that we can comfort those in any trouble
with the comfort we ourselves receive from God.
~ 2 Corinthians 1:3-4

People have chemical imbalances. This includes Christians; Christians are not excluded from having chemical imbalances just because they are Christians, just like Christians are not excluded from having heart problems or high cholesterol because they are Christians. There is not one person who takes their own life who is not experiencing some level of mental distress. Even if just temporarily, our loved one had a mental breakdown.

People want to say that real Christians do not get depressed. *"Real Christians can't get depressed because real Christians have HOPE in God."* Depression is a chemical imbalance. Sadness or "having the blues" is different from clinical depression. A person can feel depressed, which is temporary and based on their situation(s). Then there is clinical depression. There is a difference between the two.

What does all this look like? When "having the blues" and being sad, a person can still go on with their normal activities, just with feelings of sadness and melancholy. "Having the blues" is caused by life events that leave us feeling disappointed, like when we don't pass an exam in school or a date stands us up.

Clinical depression is different. The Mayo Clinic defines clinical depression as when the symptoms are *"severe enough to cause noticeable problems in relationships with others or in day-to-day activities, such as work, school or social activities."* (We will talk about depression more in a later week.)

> *But because of his great love for us,*
> *God, who is rich in mercy, made us alive with Christ*
> *even when we were dead in transgressions—*
> *it is by grace you have been saved.*
> ~ Ephesians 2:4-5

During this time of suicide grief, it is easy to understand why we doubt our faith. The unanswered questions alone create doubt towards God. God has big shoulders and can handle our anger, our questions, and the painful road we travel. He wants us to cry out to Him in the moments of anger, questions, anguish, and despair. Go ahead and yell at God. Be angry and upset. He can handle it! He doesn't mind us expressing how we feel towards Him.

He loves us and wants us to have joy and peace. God doesn't want us to be miserable on this earth. He has such great grace and mercy for us.

Teach us to number our days,
that we may gain a heart of wisdom.
~ Psalm 90:12

We, the suicide loss survivors, have a purpose for living. We must go on. Push Through. We may find an outlet for the pain that totally surprises us. Maybe we start volunteering at the local dog shelter once a month because our loved one really loved rescue dogs. Or we plant a garden, even though we have always killed any plant we had, because our loved one was always emphasizing the goodness of fresh vegetables. Or you may head up a weekly meeting for other grieving parents who lost their child to suicide or overdose.

In our grief journey, we find a new path – a path we never knew existed. In time and with healing, we can begin to know and understand that God is at work in our lives. God has not abandoned or forsaken us at all.

But blessed is the one who trusts in the Lord,
whose confidence is in him.
~ Jeremiah 17:7

TRUSTING GOD

TRUST

noun – reliance on the integrity, strength, ability, surety, etc. of a person or thing; confidence; confident expectation of something; hope (Dictionary.com)

Suicide teaches us that life is uncertain. Those left behind after a suicide tend to question everything and everyone. We don't trust. We live in a constant state of unanswered questions. And we lose trust in God.

We had no control over what our loved one did. I am sure every one of us would have stopped the suicide. But we are not in control. We cannot control anyone or anything. Yes, we can control what we eat for lunch, but we can't control the person who rear-ended us on the way to work this morning. We must let go of the thought that we had the ability or control to stop our loved one from dying by suicide.

Trust is a place of surrender. We become vulnerable in trusting God. Becoming vulnerable is not so easy to do while experiencing a suicide loss. Suicide shows us the necessity of hope and trust as we see the need to trust God with our pain. God will guide us. Read Psalm 23. We must surrender our pain and hopelessness to trust God's healing. In Him, we have hope.

Some people will feel betrayed by God in this trauma of losing their loved one to suicide. God is always there for us. He is just waiting for us to reach out to Him. God grieves with us as we grieve our loved one. God grieved with our loved one.

The LORD is compassionate and gracious,
slow to anger, abounding in love.
~ Psalm 103:8

Surely he took up our pain and bore our suffering . . .
~ Isaiah 53:4a

But you, God, see the trouble of the afflicted;
you consider their grief and take it in hand.
~ Psalm 10:14a

Jesus is beside us, carrying us in our grief. Do we trust Him to carry us? Do we trust God with our grief and pain? I must trust that God knows what is best for my life. He knows my future. He knows what lies ahead for me. God knows things that I will never know. He knows why or what led to suicide for our loved one. We must trust Him with our broken hearts, our wavering souls, and the grief that threatens to overcome us. Trust!

For in the day of trouble he will keep me safe in his dwelling;
he will hide me in the shelter of his sacred tent
and set me high upon a rock.
~ Psalm 27:5

Trust in him at all times, you people;
pour out your hearts to him,
for God is our refuge.
~ Psalm 62:8

Our trust with God is not the only place trust is lost. It is also lost amongst family and friends. We are afraid to be vulnerable. As we learn to trust God, we will also learn to trust others. It takes time, but trust can be restored. With our trust in God, we will heal, and there can be restoration in our relationships with others as we learn to trust again.

Maybe you are wondering about all of this discussion of God and eternal life and heaven. Maybe you have questions and don't understand what it means to really know Jesus. Friend, let me share this with you: God loves you and me. He wants you and me to have peace, hope, and a full, joyful life through Him.

God sent His son Jesus Christ to earth. Jesus Christ died on the cross and rose from the grave. By dying on that cross, Jesus Christ paid the penalty for our sin. God's gift of salvation is free.

Your first step towards salvation is to admit you're a sinner. Believe Jesus Christ died for you on the cross. Then ask for the forgiveness of your sins. Be willing to turn away from your sin by putting forth the effort to not sin.

You will receive Jesus Christ into your life and your heart by saying a prayer like this: *"Dear Lord, I am a sinner. I want a do-over. I want a better life that has You in it. I ask for Your forgiveness. I believe You died on the cross for my sins and rose from the dead. I trust You and will follow You as my Lord and Savior all the rest of my days on this earth. I need Your guidance. I want to do Your will. In Your name, Amen."*

It is just that simple. So, if you don't have that relationship with Jesus Christ, please consider starting that relationship right now.

HOMEWORK

1 – Has your view of God changed since your loved one died by suicide? How?

2 – Write a letter to God with your feelings. Do you feel He has let you down? Do you feel He has betrayed you? Are you angry, discouraged, untrusting, sad, grateful, relieved? Let it out.

3 – How has God been present in your grief?

4 – Look at your loved one's death through the eyes of God. What does that look like? Do you and God view your loved one and their death the same way? Journal about this.

5 – Find a spiritual accountability partner, prayer partner, or Bible study partner whom you trust and with whom you can be yourself, without judgment. *As iron sharpens iron, so one person sharpens another.* ~ Proverbs 27:17

Practical Encouragement

When feeling a little down, read the Psalms. Take time to be still and listen to what God says. Pray a Psalm daily. Maybe find one line or two that you can memorize and use as a "breath prayer" throughout the day (breathe in through a word or phrase, breathe out through a word or phrase).

WEEK 8

Patience
Hopelessness, Hope

PATIENCE

noun – the quality of being patient, as the bearing of provocation, annoyance, misfortune, or pain, without complaint, loss of temper, irritation, or the like; an ability or willingness to suppress restlessness or annoyance when confronted with delay; quiet, steady perseverance; even-tempered care; diligence (Dictionary.com)

> *Patience and fortitude conquer all things.*
> ~ Ralph Waldo Emerson

"Patient" is not a word that is in my dictionary of life. I know I should be patient, but I struggle with it. I often joke and say that the four-letter word "wait" is another word for patience – and, as we all know, four-letter words are curse words. Ha! It has become evident in my grief process that I want to be healed and done with this healing very quickly. But, life just doesn't work that way. Especially when it comes to grief.

Be patient with yourself in this process. Healing does not happen quickly. You must Push Through the grief. Don't get frustrated with yourself about your progression through this unique grief. It is a grief like no other. If you have experienced other types of grief, you will probably suffer even more as you struggle to understand why this grief is so "different." We live in an "instant gratification" world, and there is nothing instant about suicide grief.

I thought I could describe a state; make a map of sorrow.
Sorrow, however, turns out to be not a state but a process.
~ C.S. Lewis

Patience. How do we get patience? Take the time to just sit. You don't have to be on the go all the time. Be patient that you may take three steps forward and then two steps back. Be patient with this grief process. When you feel you are becoming impatient, pray. Breathe deep!

For there is a time and a way for everything,
although man's trouble lies heavy on him.
~ Ecclesiastes 8:6 (ESV)

Be patient with others. Most people don't know how to handle this – this type of grief, the circumstances around the grief, the aftermath of the grief, the suicide itself. Have patience with everyone you cross paths with. People do not know what to say or do, so they usually say nothing and do nothing. Or they may say the wrong thing or do the wrong thing. Be patient with their words and actions, as they may be slow to come.

Trust in the LORD with all your heart,
and do not lean on your own understanding.
In all your ways acknowledge him,
and he will make straight your paths.
~ Proverbs 3:5-6 (ESV)

Be patient with God. We do not understand His ways. God's timing is not our timing. We will come out of this better because of what we learn through the experience. Surrender the experience to God. He is in control. We can control the steps to mourn properly, but we can't control what life throws at us – just as we could not control our loved one and that they chose to die.

Great feats come out of wretched disaster.
~ Anonymous

Not only so, but we also glory in our sufferings,
because we know that suffering produces perseverance;
perseverance, character; and character, hope.
And hope does not put us to shame,
because God's love has been poured out into our hearts
through the Holy Spirit, who has been given to us.
~ Romans 5:3-5

Greater compassion results from suffering.
~ Anonymous

With patience, the possibility of transformation exists. In suicide loss, it's about the resilience to keep moving forward even if everything is against our moving forward – our surroundings, the suicide itself, the unanswered questions, the medical examiner's report, the unknown of the future, the messiness of emotions, the isolation, the stages of this grief, and the loss of friends and family (your tribe/your people/your support system). Give yourself patience in the resilience of getting up, over and over, and putting one foot in front of another. Push Through.

"Peace I leave with you; my peace I give to you.
Not as the world gives do I give to you.
Let not your hearts be troubled, neither let them be afraid."
~John 14:27 (ESV)

HOPELESSNESS, HOPE

HOPELESSNESS
noun – having no expectation of good or success (despairing); not susceptible to remedy or cure; incapable of redemption or improvement; giving no reason to expect good or success; giving no ground for hope (desperate); incapable of solution, management, or accomplishment (impossible) (Merriam-Webster Dictionary)

Due to the suicide loss, even if just temporarily, we have lost some of our light, joy, energy, hope, drive for life, personality, ability to trust others, etc. This "grief fog" is normal after any loss. "Grief fog" is when you can't focus, your energy is low, you are not able to make decisions, and you feel disconnected from everything and everyone. You won't be able to recall this period of "grief fog." I honestly cannot tell you what I did during my "fog" period.

So many thoughts and days were filled with hopelessness. *"How will I go on without him? He was not only the love of my life but also my best friend."* I had no hope of healing, moving forward, or even knowing where my next breath was coming from. I was lost. I was stunned. I was speechless. I was numb. I felt like someone had stepped on my air hose to life. Color was absent. I couldn't taste. I couldn't smell. I could not feel when I touched something. My vision was blurry. I hurt from the top of my head to my toes. I hurt from the inside out. I really could not see where tomorrow would come from, if it would come at all.

I was in this "grief fog" – this hopelessness – for about 100 days after my boyfriend's death. Even though I KNEW that God is my answer in all things and that He was the redeemer of all my grief, I had to experience this hopelessness to move forward – to get to the next step, which was full of every hope I could imagine.

Give your burdens to the Lord. He will carry them.
~ Psalm 55:22a (TLB – The Living Bible)

You may not start your "grief fog" until later – not immediately after the death. You may be in your "grief fog" for a couple weeks or for an extended period of time. With suicide loss, it seems like the "grief fog" lasts longer than in other types of loss. We are all different in how this journey is traveled, and that is okay.

While in your "fog," don't make any big decisions (AKA "grief decisions"). Try to hold off for a year to 18 months before making any big decisions like moving, getting remarried, selling your possessions, starting a new romance, quitting your job, buying big ticket items, etc. Grief decisions will be regretted once your "fog" has dissipated. Be aware. Do you feel a little out of control in decision-making? Find an accountability partner that you trust who can rope you in if needed.

HOPE
noun – the feeling that what is wanted can be had or that events will turn out for the best; grounds for this feeling in an instance; a person or thing in which expectations are centered; something that is hoped for (Dictionary.com)
IDIOMS
hope against hope – to continue to hope, although the outlook does not warrant it (Dictionary.com)

Hope comes from the Lord. My hope came from His promises and healing in the midst of my feelings of hopelessness.

Hope keeps us moving through grief and pain. Hope helps us look ahead and not behind. We have hope in finding simple joys in life, and in regaining a desire to live and not just exist in this life. I began, again, to experience simple things like the sound of birds chirping, seeing the golden sun setting, and hearing children laughing. Once again, life was in bright colors!

Before my boyfriend died, I had made several attempts to run a 100-mile race. This is a huge goal that takes a lot of time and effort. After my boyfriend's death, I gained a new desire to finish a 100-mile race. I had a renewed hope in achieving my goals. I had one failed attempt after his death – but, two years after his death, I did it! I got my 100-mile race completed. My renewed hope – because of his memory – is what drove me to train and accomplish my goal. I know he would have been so proud of me.

With hope comes purpose. Hope drives our desire to live again. We need to strive for really living life! Smell the roses. Eat that dessert. Hug others. We will come out of this grieving process wanting more out of life, living each day to its fullest, and having a heart of gratitude like never before.

Hope will help you find and thrive in a new normal. I didn't want a new normal. I was happy with the way things were before the suicide. But, with my renewed hope, I have found along the journey that I have an unusual hunger for the newness that is ahead. I almost get excited now. Almost.

But rejoice inasmuch you participate in the sufferings of Christ,
so that you may be overjoyed when his glory is revealed.
~ 1 Peter 4:13

When we can rest in God's grace and love, we have the eternal hope of seeing our loved one again. A smile comes all over my heart as I know I will see my boyfriend again.

I remain confident of this:
I will see the goodness of the LORD in the land of the living.
Wait for the LORD;
be strong and take heart and wait for the LORD.
~ Psalm 27:13-14

There is joy in finding peace, hope, and purpose in any circumstances, no matter how difficult. Joy comes from the Lord. Our joy will be restored even though, in the midst of this storm, it is hard to understand the journey or believe we will ever have joy again.

The righteous perish, and no one takes it to heart;
the devout are taken away, and no one understands
that the righteous are taken away to be spared from evil.
Those who walk uprightly enter into peace;
they find rest as they lie in death.
~ Isaiah 57:1-2

Those who sow with tears will reap with songs of joy.
Those who go out weeping, carrying seed to sow,
will return with songs of joy, carrying sheaves with them.
~ Psalm 126:5-6

As much as we don't want to or as hard as it is, we need to be in relationship with others during this grieving. We will gain hope when we have healthy relationships with others. Others can support us, encourage us, be an accountability partner, make us laugh, listen to us, provide a shoulder to cry on, and simply just be there for us. This is a lonely grief journey, and it helps to have someone to soldier on with.

Hope gives us security in our grief journey, empowering us to help someone else. We may be more apt to reach out to others who experience loss due to suicide. We can offer them an understanding of this unique grief. With hope comes purpose.

It does me no good to worry about things
that are impossible to know.
~ Albert Hsu

Let nothing disturb thee. Let nothing dismay thee.
All things pass; God never changes.
Patience attains all that it strives for.
He who has God finds he lacks nothing.
God alone suffices.
~ St. Teresa of Avila
God be praised, that to believing souls,
gives light in darkness, comfort in despair.
~ William Shakespeare, *Henry IV Part 2*

Godly healing comes from admitting our anger and acknowledging our grief, all accompanied by prayer. Prayer is huge for our healing. In order to heal, we need prayer, scripture, and the power and comfort that can only come from God. God is our healer! Through our prayer life, we will sense the hope that is needed to move forward.

You can find relief from the challenging emotions during your healing journey by writing a letter to your loved one, going to the grave of your loved one, talking to others, journaling, joining a grief group, exercising, praying, seeing a counselor, or moving forward in your new purpose. In healing, hope is revealed.

Hope to forge ahead and to Push Through. Keep taking one step after another.

HOMEWORK

1 – Do you feel you have grown in patience with yourself, others, and/or God? Where do you still need to grow in patience? Write a letter to God about your patience and how He wants it to be in your life.

2 – What are your top three emotions right now? Journal about them.

3 – What new hopes have you been given as time has passed in your grief? Where do you want to search to gain new hope? Journal about those areas you discover that do give you hope.

4 – What is your purpose? What did God create you to do?

5 – Peace, hope, and purpose: journal how these three go hand in hand.

Practical Encouragement

Go sit. Be still. Meditate. Listen to God. Be quiet. It requires patience to listen to God, and patience takes practice.

Find a Bible verse that inspires HOPE in you. Memorize it, meditate on it, and cling to it.

WEEK 9

The Questions

noun – a sentence worded or expressed so as to elicit information (Lexico.com)

verb – ask questions of (someone), especially in an official context (Lexico.com)

Doesn't it seem like the questions never end? We have questions that we want to ask our loved one who died by suicide. We have questions that get asked of us. We have questions we want to ask the last person who talked to or texted with our loved one. We have questions we want to ask the medical examiner. We have questions for our pastor. We have questions for our family members. We have questions for ourselves. We have questions for the community.

You will have questions until you realize what to do with them. And asking what to do with the questions is a question as well. It just seems that the journey is paved with question marks.

Here are some of the questions you may have:

Why?
Why did they do it when they told me they wouldn't?
Why did my loved one leave me?
How can I make it without my loved one?
What could I have done differently so there would have been a different outcome?
God, were you with my loved one when they took their life?
How will I pay my bills?
Was my love not enough?

Why didn't my loved one tell me what was going on with them?
What is the purpose of this?
Was I neglectful?
Where do I go from here?
What is next in my life?
Didn't my loved one know I cared?
Why didn't my loved one feel like they could trust me with their thoughts?
We were connected. We had a history. What about us? No more us.
Will I ever be over this pain?
How will I pay for the funeral?
Why did I miss "the signs"?
What were the signs anyway?
Who spoke to my loved one last?
Who saw my loved one last?
Why didn't I take my loved one seriously?
Did I do enough for my loved one?
Where is God?
Did my loved one know how much I loved them?
Did my loved one not love me?
Why don't other people in the family feel the way I do?
Why now?
Why didn't I take them to rehab one more time?
Why did they lie to me?
How could he not know how much I love him and miss him?
I think about him all the time. Where is he?
Why do people ignore me?
Will I ever stop crying?
Is he ok?
Does he need me?
Why doesn't he let me know he is ok?
Can he see me suffering and my heart breaking?
Does he remember me?
Will my sadness ever end?
When will others be okay with me talking about my loved one?

We all experience the "If only" statements:

If only I had done things differently.
If only I had paid better attention.
If only I had not gotten into an argument with my loved one.
If only I had taken him/her more seriously.
If only I had not turned my back on them.
If only I had taken them to rehab or to see a doctor.
If only I had been a better mother / father / spouse / friend / partner
   / cousin / aunt / uncle / brother / sister / grandmother
   /grandfather / neighbor / co-worker / etc.

> *I would like to add my definition of hell –*
> *it's going through life without answers.*
> ~ Deborah Chamberlain

"WHY" questions only focus on things out of our control. This is negative thinking. Think about it: there is very little we have control over. We can control what we will wear today, but we can't control the hurricane brewing off the coast that may cause grave danger to the coastal area. We must accept that we cannot control everything. Therefore, we may not have the answers to the "why" questions.

"WHAT" questions increase our ability to become more self-aware. This is positive thinking. Most "what" questions have true and accurate answers or positive possibilities. *"What will I do today, since I am off work?" "What would my loved one want me to do to honor them?"*

Dwelling on the *"Why"*s and *"If only"*s leads to bitterness and misery, which leads to burdens for us. We may never know the answers, or only receive partial answers, on this side of eternity. God has all the answers. God IS the answer. We must trust the Lord, put our faith in Him, and seek His purpose for our lives in this journey – this journey without questions answered.

It is normal to have questions. It is almost like a hunger: we need to find a reason for the suicide. We will have questions for a season of this journey. At some point in time, we will feel satisfied, and the hunger pains – the "famished" feeling – will end.

I can't tell you when that switch will flip for you. We are all different. But I do know that we will need to try to let the questions go. It took me about a year, but I learned that letting go of the questions gave me great peace and freedom. The constant desire to have answers to the endless questions was over.

Unanswered questions can keep you in an emotional and often physical jail. We dig, search, seek, ask, and feel imprisoned in the search. It can be all-consuming to hang on to those questions. It can control your life. We will go to great lengths in search of those answers. We lose sleep. We can't concentrate at work. Relationships fall to the wayside. Our health deteriorates. Our family is hurt by our lack of attention. We get caught up in an unhealthy, hostage way of life when searching for answers. Questions own us.

Again, it is normal to go through this phase of endless questions. Go through it. Push Through. Just don't dwell on the questions and remain there too long. To continue to ask the questions over and over and over will make you feel crazy, out of control, and desperate. It can disrupt your entire life, since all you can think about are the questions and the lack of answers. You may have to make the decision to Push Through this phase. You may need someone to help you see when it is time to Push Through this phase. This is where your accountability partner comes into play. Let them help you.

Our inability to find the answers to our questions may make us angry at God. Then we may end up not going to church, or we may stop praying and reading our Bible. We might even lash out at Him verbally. We feel disconnected from God. We feel abandoned – not only by our loved one who is no longer with us, but by God as well. Then we question everything about God and His love for us.

But God can handle our anger, questions, doubts, and fears. He has big shoulders to carry our burdens. He knows us, so He knows we are going to have these feelings. It's okay! Don't feel guilty because you are angry at God about your unanswered questions.

We can know by our faith that God has a plan and a purpose. We can trust Him with that better plan, even if we do not have the answers to our questions.

"For I know the plans I have for you," declares the LORD,
"plans to prosper you and not to harm you,
plans to give you hope and a future."
~ Jeremiah 29:11

We don't have the right to judge God for not giving us the answers to all our questions. He understands our frustration and pain. He loves us so much that He proved His love on the cross. It may be in our best interest to not have the answers. He may be protecting us.

My boyfriend's parents did not allow me to go to his funeral. I was a little upset and sad that I could not mourn with them, since they loved him like I did. But I changed my perspective and realized that God may have been saving me from further heartache I might have encountered if I had been there. Yes, it hurt that I was kept from being there. But, He knows, and I trust Him. I let it go. I gave up the questions about why I wasn't wanted there at the funeral.

You may not only be angry with God about not getting answers. You may also get angry with others and yourself. I feel our expectations and perceptions have a direct impact on how we deal with our questions and any answers we may receive. If I am expecting the last person my boyfriend spoke with before he took his life to have all of the answers to my *"why"*s, *"where"*s, *"what"*s, *"who"*s, *"when"*s, and *"how"*s, I am probably setting myself up to be disappointed and let down. I may get some of those answers, or I may not. I may get angry at this person because they are not giving me what I think they should give me.

Your situation is probably different than mine. But try to think about how an attitude/heart change on your part may eliminate the angry feelings and disappointing expectations. I recommend lots of prayer when an attitude/ heart change needs to take place.

Remember: the answer to the question is not always what you want. So, if it isn't what you want, do you disregard that answer and just keep on asking until you get the answer you want? Then, let's say you do get an answer you agree with. Does it change the question or the reason for the question? No and No. Is there just one answer to a question, or can there be more than one answer? Possibly. Don't perception and interpretation have a lot to do with answers? Yes.

If I get an answer to any of my questions, does it change anything? No. My loved one is still dead. The answer does not bring my loved one back. What do answers really change? Does an answer bring peace? Maybe the answer to a question would be way more painful than my hurt in not having the answer. So, do I really need that answer? I must trust that my not knowing those answers may be a protection for me. And I am pretty sure that when I get to heaven, I probably won't care to have those questions answered.

Do I really need the answers to move on and heal? No. I have learned that my healing comes faster and that I can move forward more quickly if I let the questions go. I have learned that I could not have peace or freedom until I let the questions go. I have peace in knowing I am okay without the answers. I trust. I have hope. And the answers to the questions will have no bearing on that trust and hope I carry in my heart!

Maybe it will help you to say this simple prayer:

"Lord, I don't understand. Help me to trust You and Your ways."

We feel like we need reassurance that we are not the reason for the suicide. Only the person who died by suicide has a clue of the real reasons why. Even if a note is left, it will more than likely contain only what the person wanted those left behind to believe. The note will never tell the whole story. So, don't think a note has all the answers. Try not to put much "faith" in the note, if there was one.

Our loved one was so focused on escaping the pain and despair that they were not aware how the act of suicide would cause untold grief for those left behind. It was not selfish of our loved one to die by suicide. Our loved one felt like a burden, so if anything, it was selfless: they wanted to not be a burden to us. We know that they were not a burden. But that is how they felt. Their act of suicide was irrational. We can't make sense of it.

We search for a precise event that caused the suicide. We think the act of suicide will cease to be incomprehensible if we can identify the cause of the suicide, but there is never one reason why a person takes their life. The reasons are as deep as they are wide. Suicide results from a complex interaction of many factors and usually involves a history of psychological problems. The psychological issue could be mixed with a permanent or a temporary chemical imbalance. An example of a psychological issue mixed with a chemical imbalance would be a mixture of depression and alcohol/drug addiction. There is no rational reason for suicide. You are not the reason for the suicide.

In our minds, we equate explanations with comfort. This is false. We don't need the *"why"* answered to heal our broken heart. God will heal our broken heart. It is not easy to let go of the *"why"*'s or any of the questions that have consumed our being, but letting go of the *"why"* is one of the first steps in healing.

Just imagine your loved one saying this to you:

"Hey, I love you. I am sorry I am not with you any longer. Please try to think about me when I was at my best and we shared good times together. Keep our memories close to your heart. I hope they bring you a smile. Go enjoy your life to the fullest. Have the best experiences you can. Laugh often. Make new memories that bring a smile to your heart. I am sorry. My decision to end my life had nothing to do with you. I just couldn't take the pain any longer. You will find comfort in God. Draw closer to God. He loves you, and so do I."

Eventually, the questions change:

How can I turn this event into a way to help others?
Lord, what do you want me to do with this experience?
Who needs a word of hope or encouragement today?
How can my mourning turn into joy?
Where can I help others?
How can I honor my loved one?
How can I lessen the pain of others?
What can I gain that is positive from this?

The *"could have"*s, *"should have"*s, and *"what if"*s – you have to give up the search for these answers and let it go so you can move forward. Push Through. Release these questions to God. Ask God to remove them from your heart. Ask for a heart change, perspective change, and/or attitude change.

HOMEWORK

1 – Of the questions we discussed today, which ones still haunt you? If you could get the answers, how would it make you feel?

2 – Let it Go! What do you need to surrender to God? What questions do you have for God? Write Him a letter.

3 – How do you feel about letting the questions go and not needing to have the answers? Do you have an accountability partner to help you recognize when it's time to let go and Push Through? Reach out to them about this.

4 – How can you turn your experience with suicide loss grief into a way to help others? Ask the Lord what He wants you to do with this experience.

5 – Who needs a word of hope or encouragement today? Seek them out and be the encourager.

Practical Encouragement

Get quiet. Sit in silence. Slow down. This is inside-out healing. You will need to practice being still.

Fresh air is good for you. Try to get outside for about 20 minutes each day to get some natural vitamin D.

WEEK 10

Trauma
PTSD
Depression

This week's topics are for the person who has lost someone due to suicide or overdose, not the person that has attempted suicide.

Experiencing trauma, depression, and often PTSD after losing someone we love to suicide or overdose is not uncommon.

I had some previous knowledge about trauma and PTSD due to my education background. During this experience in my life, I have dug into trauma and PTSD a little deeper and found some of the following information by exploring different sources: www.ncbi.nlm.nih.gov, WebMD, and Mayo Clinic.

TRAUMA

noun – the response to a deeply distressing or disturbing event that overwhelms an individual's ability to cope, causes feelings of helplessness, diminishes their sense of self and their ability to feel the full range of emotions and experiences. It does not discriminate. (Integratedlistening.com)

You have experienced a trauma if you have lost someone to suicide or overdose. The trauma you feel may be heightened if you were the one who found your loved one or if you witnessed the life-ending event of your loved one. It can feel overwhelming as you try to get these traumatic images out of your mind.

117

The trauma of any type of sudden death holds a person in complete emotional, physical, and mental hell. It is unexpected. We are in shock. We have no control over this.

With a suicide, the normal feelings typically associated with death may be more prolonged and more intense. Suicide feels like it is a double whammy. The shock, stigma, shame, guilt, disconnectedness, unanswered questions, rejection, and feelings of abandonment with a suicide make the trauma deep and more intense. Anxiety, despair, and disbelief create a magnified trauma for those of us who have experienced loss due to suicide. We already know this grief is "different" – now, the side effects of the trauma are also "different."

Just what does experiencing trauma look like? At first there is *"'Psychic numbing' and/or 'emotional anesthesia'. This is when you are not able to recall important aspects of a traumatic event. This is followed by feelings of detachment or estrangement from others, loss of interest in events that used to be enjoyed, and inability to feel emotions of any kind, especially intimacy, sexuality, or tenderness"* (Cliffsidemalibu.com).

These feelings are not conscious feelings, but rather subconscious. Some people do make choices in the numbing phase and choose to use alcohol and/or drugs to numb the pain. Alcohol and/or drugs are not good options for dealing with trauma. Choose healthy ways to deal with trauma.

At first, you need to remember the basics. Learn how to breathe with purpose. Try relaxing. Get some fresh air. Exercise. Go see a pastor or a counselor. Spend time with a good friend or group of friends. It takes time to sort through the experience of a traumatic event. Be patient in the recovery.

The trauma of suicide can lead to PTSD (Post-Traumatic Stress Disorder) for the ones who are left behind after a suicide loss.

PTSD

There is a great chance that, because of the trauma you have experienced in losing your loved one to suicide, you will experience PTSD. Please understand that this is not a weakness on your part. It's physiological. You are not a bad person because of experiencing PTSD. Please seek medical help if you think you have symptoms of PTSD. Only a medical diagnosis can determine if you have PTSD.

What is PTSD? According to Mayo Clinic, *"PTSD is a mental health condition that is triggered by a terrifying event – either experiencing the event or witnessing the event."*

PTSD is more profound in man-made disasters versus natural disasters. If a hurricane destroys your home, that is not a choice situation. Your loved one chose to take their life. We had no choice in our loved one's death by suicide. Suicide would be considered a man-made disaster, while a forest fire or an earthquake is a natural disaster.

Rarely does one terrifying event alone create PTSD. Multiple tragic deaths may bring forth delayed reactions from a prior tragic death. The coupled tragic deaths can create the perfect storm and bring on PTSD.

I lost my boyfriend in 2016. I didn't experience the symptoms of PTSD in my grieving journey. I was thankful. In the summer of 2018, I lost my uncle during a tragic event. My uncle had a massive heart attack while in the water at a lake. Then, within 48 hours, I discovered that a dear friend had also died tragically from a pulmonary embolism. My friend had been soaking in the bathtub because his legs hurt so bad.

I was devastated to experience these two losses so close together. Having two tragic losses within 48 hours seemed to bring forth the trauma from losing my boyfriend to suicide. I started having some PTSD symptoms two years after my boyfriend died, not immediately after his death. I did seek the help I needed from my primary care physician and my counselor.

There are no specific guidelines when it comes to the exact way each of our brains is affected by traumatic events. Each person reacts differently. Not everyone processes traumatic events the same way, and not everyone will experience PTSD. You and I can witness the same traumatic event and respond in very different ways. There is no right or wrong. It just is what it is, for each of us. We each have to take the path we are on and learn to Push Through.

PTSD can happen to anyone. Several factors can increase the chance that someone will have PTSD, many of which are not under that person's control. Stress, experiencing multiple traumatic events, and genetic predispositions can all increase the chances of PTSD. There isn't a list of "approved" traumatic events that cause PTSD. PTSD has no boundaries. It is NOT a sign of weakness.

Talking about the traumatic event right after the traumatic event and getting counseling can help decrease the chances of a person experiencing PTSD. But, remember: sometimes, we take vitamin C and eat right but still manage to get a nasty cold. We can do everything we know to do for prevention, but sometimes, our body will do what it has to do to process our loss.

He will cover you with his feathers,
and under his wings you will find refuge;
his faithfulness will be your shield and rampart.
You will not fear the terror of night,
nor the arrow that flies by day,
nor the pestilence that stalks in the darkness,
nor the plague that destroys at midday.
~ Psalm 91:4-6

According to WebMD, the following are symptoms of PTSD:

Nightmares/Flashbacks – *Traumatic memories can visit you in sleep as nightmares or as flashbacks during the day. You may feel as if you are reliving the traumatic event for the first time. The nightmares or flashbacks may cause you to feel afraid, anxious, guilty, or suspicious. Physically you may experience chills, shaking, headaches, heart palpitations, and panic attacks.*

Avoidance – *You will stay away from places, people, activities or anything that reminds you of the suicide event. You may even find yourself staying away from people all together. You feel disconnected.*

Behavior changes – *You may not be yourself due to intense emotional feelings. You may find it hard to stay focused or to concentrate. Your normal life will not be normal any longer.*

Mood swings – *You may feel all over the place in everything you do. Everything feels negative. You have feelings of numbness, sadness, depression, and hopelessness, and you are not interested in the events you used to be interested in.*

Other side effects of PTSD:

~ experiencing negative beliefs and feelings
~ changed perspective of yourself and others
~ guilt and shame
~ lost interest in things you used to enjoy
~ feeling the world is dangerous
~ distrust of others
~ feeling keyed up, jittery, easily startled
~ always being on the alert for the next bad event to happen

PTSD can look different to each person who experiences PTSD. You may not have sound sleep. It may be a chore to complete tasks. Concentration may be difficult. You may feel numb. You may lose all sense of joy or happiness. You may feel angry and irritable. You may start excessive unhealthy lifestyle experiences like smoking, overeating, driving recklessly, doing drugs, or consuming too much alcohol. You may start to behave totally out of character compared to your life before PTSD.

The LORD is my shepherd, I lack nothing.
He makes me lie down in green pastures,
he leads me beside quiet waters,
he refreshes my soul.
He guides me along the right paths for his name's sake.
Even though I walk through the darkest valley,
I will fear no evil, for you are with me;
your rod and your staff, they comfort me.
You prepare a table before me in the presence of my enemies.
You anoint my head with oil; my cup overflows.
Surely your goodness and love will follow me
all the days of my life,
and I will dwell in the house of the LORD forever.
~ Psalm 23:1-6

It's NORMAL to have upsetting memories, feel on edge, or have trouble sleeping after experiencing loss due to suicide. At first, it may be hard to do normal daily activities – going to work, going to school, spending time with people you care about – but most people start to feel better after a few weeks or months. If it's been longer than a few months and you're still having symptoms, you may have PTSD.

For some people, PTSD symptoms may start later, or they may come and go over time. Long-lasting symptoms of PTSD are disturbing nightmares and/or flashbacks, insomnia, hyperarousal, and/or anxiety. PTSD is complicated, just like our grief.

*Then they cried to the L*ORD *in their trouble,*
and he saved them from their distress.
He brought them out of darkness, the utter darkness,
and broke away their chains.
*Let them give thanks to the L*ORD *for his unfailing love*
and his wonderful deeds for mankind,
for he breaks down gates of bronze
and cuts through bars of iron.
~ Psalm 107:13-16

My brain is at war again
and the odd detachment between the memories and hurt.
I'm not crying outwardly but in my mind I can hear myself wailing
and another part attempting to pacify the first.
I feel insane, I feel every emotion and none.
I feel disconnected and wholly present.
I feel impotent.
~ Unknown

"I will repay you for the years the locusts have eaten—
the great locust and the young locust,
the other locusts and the locust swarm—
my great army that I sent among you."
~ Joel 2:25

Loss due to suicide is harder to recover from if you have to go it alone. Without talking to others, it becomes even harder to understand the suicide (why), the guilt, the shame, the stigma, and the silence. Get into a group where you can share with one another. Counseling coupled with group therapy is most beneficial.

Therapeutic ways to treat PTSD, according to the Mayo Clinic, are the following:

Cognitive therapy – *talk therapy that helps you recognize the ways of thinking (cognitive patterns) that are keeping you stuck*
Exposure therapy – *This behavioral therapy helps you safely face both situations and memories that you find frightening so that you can learn to cope with them effectively. This therapy can be particularly helpful for flashbacks and nightmares.*
Eye movement desensitization and reprocessing (EMDR) – *EMDR combines exposure therapy with a series of guided eye movements that help you process traumatic memories and change how you react to them.*

A little more about EMDR:

"EMDR therapy is an eight-phase treatment and involves attention to three time periods: the past, the present, and the future. Focus is given to past disturbing memories and related events." (EMDR Institute, Inc)

I know people who have experienced traumatic events in their life who have had success by utilizing EMDR. This is a newer method of treating traumas, but I have heard rave reviews from those who have tried this method of treatment.

DEPRESSION

noun – an act of depressing or a state of being depressed, such as a state of feeling sad; a mood disorder marked especially by sadness, inactivity, difficulty in thinking and concentration, a significant increase or decrease in appetite and time spent sleeping, feelings of dejection and hopelessness, and sometimes suicidal tendencies (Merriam-Webster Dictionary)

According to the American Psychiatric Association, depression symptoms may include the following, "from mild to severe, for at least two weeks":

~ *Feeling sad or having a depressed mood*
~ *Loss of interest or pleasure in activities once enjoyed*
~ *Changes in appetite – weight loss or gain unrelated to dieting*
~ *Trouble sleeping or sleeping too much*
~ *Loss of energy or increased fatigue*
~ *Increase in purposeless physical activity (e.g., hand-wringing or pacing) or slowed movements and speech (actions observable by others)*
~ *Feeling worthless or guilty*
~ *Difficulty thinking, concentrating or making decisions*
~ *Thoughts of death or suicide*

Depression is silence. Depression is decreased activity – mentally, emotionally, and physically. Depression debilitates you. All senses (seeing, smelling, tasting, hearing, touch) are dulled or non-existent. You may feel like you did in your "grief fog."

I waited patiently for the LORD;
he turned to me and heard my cry.
He lifted me out of the slimy pit, out of the mud and mire;
he set my feet on a rock and gave me a firm place to stand.
He put a new song in my mouth, a hymn of praise to our God.
Many will see and fear the LORD and put their trust in him.
~ Psalm 40:1-3

Humble yourselves, therefore, under God's mighty hand,
that he may lift you up in due time.
~ 1 Peter 5:6

"I have told you these things,
so that in me you may have peace.
In this world you will have trouble.
But take heart! I have overcome the world."
~ John 16:33

For I am convinced that neither death nor life,
neither angels nor demons,
neither the present nor the future, nor any powers,
neither height nor depth, nor anything else in all creation,
will be able to separate us from the love of God
that is in Christ Jesus our Lord.
~ Romans 8:38-39

So do not fear, for I am with you;
do not be dismayed, for I am your God.
I will strengthen you and help you;
I will uphold you with my righteous right hand.
~ Isaiah 41:10

Remember: depression – clinical or situational – is different than sadness or "having the blues." Clinical depression results from a chemical imbalance. Heredity and environmental factors also play a part in all mental illnesses, including depression. A person can be sad without being depressed. See a medical doctor to determine if you are suffering from clinical depression or not.

Situational depression can also be classified as "reactive" since it is based on individual events, trauma, or a trigger, like losing a job or a relationship ending. Situational depression can take place any time after a traumatic event. Possible symptoms of situational depression are avoidance, crying, disinterest, or inability to focus. (Healthline.com) You can be situationally depressed without having clinical depression, but it's still different from normal sadness or "having the blues."

126

So, what is being sad or "having the blues"? Merriam-Webster Dictionary defines "sad" as *"affected with or expressive of grief or unhappiness (downcast); causing or associated with grief or unhappiness."* Sadness tends to be situational and temporary. It is not a lasting feeling or a state of being like depression. Do you think you are sad or depressed?

"Depression usually takes place between the 3rd and 12th month after the suicide." (Wikipedia) It sets in after the "grief fog" has lifted. Depression affects the physical, mental, relational, and spiritual aspects of our lives. With depression, there is a diminished interest in life and/or no interest in what used to be pleasurable activities. There can also be significant changes in appetite – too much, too little, or no appetite at all. You may feel like you can't stay on the path, unable to complete a task or a thought. Sleeping is disrupted – you may sleep too much or suffer from insomnia. Clinically depressed people feel unworthy and have feelings of guilt.

Depression might lead to suicide ideation. Suicide ideation is when those left behind see that the deceased escaped their anguish and pains and have put an end to their suffering, so those left behind also consider suicide as a way out of their pains. *"Suicidal ideation often entails three markers: a perception of burdensomeness to others; a sense of failed belongingness; and an exposure to repeated painful and fearsome experiences that can lead to habituation with the pain and fear of self injury."* (Joiner, 2005, p. 46-47, 92-93; Shneidman, 1996, p. 129-137) A clinically depressed person may have thoughts of suicide or a belief that this life is just not worth living any longer.

With suicide, we get no opportunity to say good-bye. We feel rejected and cheated by our loved one. It's almost like there was a fight going on, and they slammed the door shut – they had the last word. We never got a chance to make things "right," say "I love you," help them, or hug them. These thoughts can lead to feelings of depression.

Depression can stem from fear and anger, especially unexpressed anger. You are afraid that a need will not be met; fear leads to anger; depression = anger turned inward. And it is easy to see why we are afraid after we lose our loved one to suicide: loneliness, stigmas, unanswered questions, guilt, and shame.

During the heavy grieving period after the suicide, those of us left behind tend to do self-destructive things. Everything is out of sorts in our life. We may get angry because we are spinning out of control in our lifestyle. We may spend too much money and end up with financial problems. We may be tempted to experience infidelity in an effort to feel better about ourselves. We may do something that is not socially acceptable, and our social community looks down on our character. Alcohol and/or drugs may interfere with the productivity of our life. These types of choices could lead to anger – which could contribute to depression.

When you are faced with words or actions that are not favorable, respond – don't react. Has anyone told you to *"get over it"* concerning your sadness or depressive disposition? I was told, *"Your boyfriend loved alcohol more than he loved you."* I was also told, *"If you had been worthy, your boyfriend would not have killed himself."* I was even told, *"His blood is on your hands."* These words were very hurtful. I remained silent in response. I didn't yell back or defend myself.

Maybe I should have responded differently, but at that time, I was depressed and just didn't have it in me to speak up or defend myself. I am a strong person and can handle ill-willed words. But I worry about other people who may be the recipient of such negativity. Those hurtful words could totally destroy someone.

128

Experience the wound, experience the shock, experience the trauma, and let it wash over you. It won't destroy you. Trust that, in time, all wounds heal. Try to feel peace that your loved one is no longer suffering. No more mental hell on this earth for your loved one. You must Push Through this journey. It's hard. It hurts. But you can do it!

Clinical or situational depression cannot be fixed by going shopping, eating a favorite meal, taking a vacation, or by dismissing it. Going to a medical doctor is where the solution lies. And it is okay for a Christian to go to a medical doctor. We don't mind going to a doctor for a broken foot or if we have a sinus infection, so we should seek medical help if we are clinically depressed.

By seeking help, it doesn't mean that we have turned our backs on God, lost our hope, or that we are unbelievers. If we go to the doctor for a bad cold, that doesn't mean we have lost hope in God or that we have lost our way. We can't let the stigmas of depression or mental illness keep us from seeking the help that we need in healing our bodies and minds.

Christians who are depressed often feel judged or rejected by their Christian friends or from the church. Feeling rejected or judged adds to the already existing pain. Christians, just like anyone else, get chemical imbalances, and they need professional help to get the imbalances straightened out. Christians can also experience situational depression as a result of trauma. It is not a character defect to be depressed. It isn't a character defect to seek help.

You are extremely fragile when healing. Healing takes place in time with proper care, plenty of rest, and gentle treatment. You are in an emotional and spiritual hell on earth. Be good to yourself. Surround yourself with others who support a healthy lifestyle for you.

I felt like I needed someone to go before me to set a protective boundary. I felt like I always needed a bodyguard to be there when I fell – to help me have a voice or make decisions. I felt alone because I didn't have a bodyguard to go before or with me on my journey. Then I realized that God goes before me. He is with me, no matter what. He is my protector. Realizing this gave me peace.

> *"The LORD himself goes before you and will be with you;*
> *he will never leave you nor forsake you.*
> *Do not be afraid; do not be discouraged."*
> ~ Deuteronomy 31:8

Make the effort to have restorative quiet time. Quiet time allows the body to restore itself. Silence clears the clutter of the mind. Being quiet allows us to listen to our own voice and to hear God's messages to us. Be careful that you know the difference between quiet time and checking out. Checking out is not productive or good for our healing. (This is where an accountability partner comes in handy.)

Did you know that helping others dispels depression? I know it is hard to get out there and get going, because you just do not feel like it. No "giddy up" is present. Still, it is important for your healing.

Get out there and help others in whatever manner you desire. You may have a gift for storytelling – go volunteer at a local library to read books to small children. Or you may have a love for older people – go volunteer at a local nursing home to paint an elderly lady's fingernails. Get your family members together and do an "Adopt a Street" outreach in your loved one's memory. Being active will help in your mood improvement process.

Community + Connection = Healing.

Talking helps alleviate depression. Talking helps sort out your feelings. Being connected to others in the community will help in your healing. You can talk with others, listen to others, volunteer, or be involved socially. For me, a combination of one-on-one counseling and group interaction with others who have suffered loss due to suicide has been beneficial in my healing and moving forward in a healthy manner.

As always, seek medical help if you feel you may be experiencing your depression in a manner beyond sadness or "feeling the blues."

"Come to me, all you who are weary and burdened,
and I will give you rest.
Take my yoke upon you and learn from me,
for I am gentle and humble in heart,
and you will find rest for your souls.
For my yoke is easy and my burden is light."
~Matthew 11:28-30

HOMEWORK

1 – Grab your journal and write about your traumatic event – the experience itself, and the after-effects.

2 – Do you think you have experienced PTSD? Have you sought professional help? Write down your experience with PTSD. Put it on paper.

3 – Have you experienced depression? Did you seek professional help? What does depression look like for you?

4 – What steps will you take if you start experiencing depression and/or PTSD? Would you consider doing EMDR as part of your healing? Why or why not?

5 – Read over these verses. Which stand out for you more than the others, and why? Journal about the verses that speak to you.

1 Peter 4:12-13	Isaiah 41:10
1 Peter 5:6	John 16:33
Romans 8:38-39	Psalm 40:1-3
Psalm 23:1-6	Matthew 11:28-30
Joel 2:25	Psalm 91:4-6
Psalm 107:13-16	

Practical Encouragement

Get out there and get 30 minutes of exercise every day this week. You pick which kind – walking, running, biking, swimming, yoga, gardening, hiking in the woods, etc. Journal after your exercise about how you feel.

Play with a dog or pet. You can be depressed, needy, and confused, but rubbing an animal's coat, talking to an animal, holding a pet, and rubbing its ears can all bring comfort. Animals are nonjudgmental and provide unconditional love.

WEEK 11

The Body
Taking Care of Yourself

I have always had a passion for taking care of my body and being physically active. It's part of my DNA to be active. My college degree is in Physical Education, and I love studying all things about the body, nutrition, and exercise. But, when I was in my initial grief fog – about 100 days – after my boyfriend died by suicide, my diet and exercise regimens suffered and even became nonexistent. I am not even sure if I ate. I don't remember.

In this journey, I have learned self-care is very important to healing. It is my responsibility to take care of all aspects of my being: mental, physical, emotional, and spiritual.

Therefore, I urge you, brothers and sisters,
in view of God's mercy,
to offer your bodies as a living sacrifice,
holy and pleasing to God—
this is your true and proper worship.
~ Romans 12:1

Do you not know that your bodies are temples of the Holy Spirit,
who is in you, whom you have received from God?
You are not your own; you were bought at a price.
Therefore honor God with your bodies.
~ 1 Corinthians 6:19-20

Dear friend, I pray that you may enjoy good health
and that all may go well with you,
even as your soul is getting along well.
~ 3 John 1:2

It is easy to let our nutrition, physical activity level, personal self-care, and anything to do with ourselves fall to the wayside when we are experiencing grief due to suicide – especially if we are caring for others who are also suffering in loss. We stop exercising. We stop going to church. We don't eat, or we eat too much. We eat the "wrong" foods. We consume too much alcohol. Our immune system gets weak. We get sick more easily. We don't sleep the number of hours we need in order to be rested.

We stop talking and sharing our thoughts and feelings with our friends/family. We end up caring for all of those around us, and we neglect our own self-care. We may have panic attacks. Our sleep is totally disturbed. We want to stay in bed. We are unmotivated. We have no energy. We are in a grief fog.

We are lost.

We don't care.

We feel numb.

We neglect every aspect of our being, which is not what we should do.

Taking care of ourselves, inside and out, is crucial in healing! An accountability partner is helpful here, as they can get you back on track in your self-care regimen.

So whether you eat or drink or whatever you do,
do it all for the glory of God.
~ 1 Corinthians 10:31

Remember: if you are experiencing depression beyond what is expected with sadness, go see your physician. Medications may be necessary at this time of your journey.

If you need to, find a counselor to talk to. If you can, find a counselor who is knowledgeable about suicide loss. Find a good support group. (You are here.) A combination of group therapy and one-on-one therapy is very beneficial. Talk, share, and let it out. There is healing in talking. Your body will feel relieved. You will be able to breathe better. Your body will experience freedom once you are taking better care of yourself.

REST. Rest is not sleeping. Be still. Get quiet. Meditate. Pray. Journal. Breathe. Listen to God. Reflect. Most people will grow closer to God during this time of grief. He is your healer – not just of your spirit, but also of your physical being, heart, and mind!

When I am experiencing a little anxiety, I must remind myself to breathe. Try this method of relaxation: inhale, count to 4 – hold, count to 4 – exhale, count to 4. Repeat 10 times. This simple breathing exercise brings me around every time. Clear your thoughts as you concentrate on the breathing. Try to feel the breath all through your body.

Try to drink more water and less soda or coffee. Don't over-consume alcohol. Make smart food choices, and eat. Remember: too much of anything is not good for you. Everything in moderation.

Go see your chiropractor. Aligning your body helps every aspect of your body. It aids in healing your body in a natural way. Get a massage. This is not only relaxing, but also healing. Make sure your massage practitioner knows what you are going through. Don't be ashamed of your grief.

Get outside. Try to be one with nature. Listen to the birds. Enjoy the scenery. Listen to a podcast or your favorite music while walking or running. Find a friend to walk with. Or just walk and talk to God – or don't talk, and listen to Him speak to you in the silence. When I am on my long runs of 15+ miles, I enjoy my time with God. I start my prayers with prayers of thanksgiving and gratitude. It makes the time go by quicker. And I feel lighter, since my time running was spent in conversation with the Lord.

Go to yoga, Pilates, or some relaxing form of exercise. Maybe your choice is swimming or going for a bike ride. We are all different and have different ways to relax and unwind.

Try to maintain a routine. Get out of bed at the same time each day. Make a daily list. Check it off as you go. It keeps you focused, and you have a sense of accomplishment for that day. Make a weekly and monthly schedule. Set goals. Check the goals off once you have achieved them.

I keep a notebook. I use it to jot down thoughts or ideas during the day. I put my shopping list in it. I keep a schedule of daily To Do lists. It helps me stay organized. I also have a work calendar that I use. Yes, it's an actual calendar. I prefer the old-fashioned way. You may want to use your smartphone for your To Do lists and calendars.

Eat a well-balanced diet. Americans are known for "emotional" eating. Don't get into bad eating habits with sodas, desserts, lots of bread, foods loaded with processed sugar, and starchy foods. Don't jump into a whole new eating lifestyle at the early stages of your grief. There are enough "new" things happening. Wait for six months to completely overhaul your eating patterns or start a whole new way of managing your nutrition.

Take vitamins and supplements. Do research. Talk to your doctor or a nutritionist to discover what your body may be lacking, what it needs, and what will make you feel better. Stress and trauma, which you are going through with suicide loss grief, change the chemicals in your physiological being. Your diet can play a big part in your mood.

Shoot for at least 30 minutes a day of cardiovascular (cardio) exercise. Cardio exercise, also known as aerobic activity, uses large muscle movement over a sustained time, keeping your heart rate to at least 50% of its maximum level.

I found the following information from the "Target Heart Rate" article at Healthstatus.com to be very helpful:

First, you need to find your resting heart rate. "Your resting heart rate is the number of times your heart beats while doing nothing. This number is determined by taking your one-minute pulse rate when you wake in the morning before getting out of bed." Take your pulse for 15 seconds, then multiply by 4. This gives you your base resting heart rate.

The National Institute of Health lists the average resting heart rate for children (10 years and older) and adults (including seniors) as 60-100 beats per minute. For athletes, the resting heart rate is 40-60 beats per minute.

To obtain your target heart rate, do the following: while exercising, STOP. Take your pulse at your neck or wrist for 15 seconds. Multiply that number by 4 to calculate your heartbeats per minute. "Moderate exercise intensity" is "50 to about 70 percent of your maximum heart rate." "Vigorous exercise intensity" is "70 to about 85 percent of your maximum heart rate."

Forms of cardiovascular exercise include running, swimming, walking, elliptical, high intensity interval weight training, rowing, cycling, stair climbing, jumping rope, and circuit training. Get that heart rate up. You can also do anaerobic activities like working in the garden, going to the gym and lifting weights, bowling, or roller skating. Find some kids and play hide-and-seek outside. Go for a hike. Fly a kite. Go hunting. Go take pictures outdoors. Move your body! You will feel better, I promise!

Guard your heart above all else,
for it determines the course of your life.
~ Proverbs 4:23 (NLT – New Living Translation)

There are other self-care ways of taking care of your mind and body. Read up on the techniques of blocking, visualization, and relaxation. Ask your counselor about coping techniques and how to apply them to your life.

I am a big believer in journaling. It clears the head and soul to put thought to paper. You can write letters to your loved one who is no longer here, your family, your friends, and yourself. You don't have to send the letters. Just write them and get those feelings and thoughts out of you. Journaling is a way of letting go. Expressing your thoughts and feelings on paper brings freedom and peace. Again, you may prefer your tablet, laptop, or smartphone.

If you can, try to take personal 2- or 3-day retreats. Taking a longer vacation soon after your loss sounds like a dream. It sounds like it could be a great escape from your day-to-day routine, environment, daily life expectations, and the grief you are experiencing. But, it will probably cause greater stress to be gone for an extended vacation too early in your grief. Too many changes too soon might increase your stress levels. Take baby steps in the changes you have control over.

If you can't leave home, plan a "staycation." You can stay at home, turn off your phone, binge watch television, read a couple books, sleep in, or do nothing. Make this a positive, uplifting staycation. Don't get wrapped up in negativity, sleeping the entire time, or binge eating. Make it clear to others that you need this time to rejuvenate. They will understand. It is okay to take care of yourself in your grief.

It is okay to ask for help from those in your tribe. You may have to force yourself to do this. It is hard to ask for help during a state of devastation. Pride also plays a part in asking for help. We think we can do it all by ourselves, but we cannot do it all by ourselves in this journey of suicide loss grief. I am sure there are people out there who have offered to help. Take them up on it. Don't block them from blessing you. Reach out to others. Humble yourself. You are loved, and others want to love on you by helping you.

Find a nonjudgmental, caring, supportive, patient friend who will be glad to listen to you and keep it confidential. Trust is difficult at this time, so make sure you feel safe with the person you share your heart with. There is healing in talking. If you feel you cannot trust a friend, see a counselor – preferably one who is knowledgeable about suicide loss grief. If this person can be your accountability partner, that is a bonus! We may need someone to keep an eye on our physical and mental being, financial decisions, and the overall process of decision-making.

Try to not be so hard that you do not allow others in your life, or so hard that you do not allow others in your heart. There are people who want to be in your life. It feels good to be someone's person. Nurture the relationships you had before the loss, and put effort into new relationships that develop after the loss.

As weird as it may seem, this may be a good time to build new relationships or to strengthen relationships that were present before the suicide loss. You will realize that nothing stays the same after experiencing the loss of your loved one to suicide. This includes your friendships and all other relationships in your life. Some change for the good. Some relationships end. You are not the same person that you were. Accept it!

Our lives can be compared to the life of a tree. Trees are planted, watered, and fertilized – just as we must take care of our whole selves if we want to grow. Trees go through the seasons of winter, spring, summer, and fall. We go through seasons as well – and you probably feel like you are in a winter in your grief.

As we know, when a tree gets its limbs trimmed, that means there will be new growth. And, in your life, you may find that you will need to cut some dead branches from your "tree." Sometimes it is hard to let go, but it is necessary for growth – if you want to see new blooms in your "spring." The positive friends and 2 a.m. friends will still be on your tree to bloom. The new friendships will also be on your tree to bloom! Keep your heart open to new relationships.

Remember, there are others who are also hurting because of your loved one's suicide. You really are not alone, even though you feel like it. If you can't connect with others who are feeling like you do about your loved one, find a support group for people who have lost someone to suicide. If there is not a support group in your area, start one. Maybe starting a support group is part of your healing. Maybe you feel compelled to help others in your grief journey. It is comforting to know others feel the same way you do at this time of your life.

Be still and know that I am God . . .
~ Psalm 46:10 (ESV)

HOMEWORK

1 – Do you feel as if you have neglected taking care of yourself? How so? What changes are you going to make?

2 – Have you been trying to stay too busy in your grief? How can you change this? How can you be purposeful about rest?

3 – Start a prayer journal. Fill it with prayers for others, prayers of thanksgiving, and your personal prayers.

4 – Have you seen a counselor? Do you think this is a good idea for you?

5 – Plan to take care of yourself: get a pedicure or a massage, start a new eating plan that is healthy, drink more water throughout your day, get outside, start a new exercise.

Practical Encouragement

Go have fun! Do an activity you have been thinking about doing.

Get outside: go for a hike, take up photography, work in the garden or yard, go for a bike ride, or just sit outside and enjoy your surroundings. Listen to nature.

If you're new to cardio exercise, start slow: go for a 10-min walk, then increase each week by 5 mins until you reach 30 mins. Then pick up the pace. While walking, think of your loved one, pray, listen to uplifting podcasts or music, or enjoy the silence.

Hug someone that you wouldn't normally hug. Touch is healing.

WEEK 12

Rejection
Regret
Relief

The three R's of suicide loss grief: Rejection. Regret. Relief. These three do not seem to be grouped together in other types of grief. Just with this one.

REJECTION

noun – the dismissing or refusing of a proposal, idea, etc.; the spurning of a person's affections (Lexico.com)

Do you feel like your loved one pulled the ultimate act of rejection by taking their own life? Or do you feel like people in your life have rejected you because your loved one died by suicide? Do you feel like society rejected you because your loved one died by suicide? Or maybe you are rejecting every suggestion, all offers of help, or the people in your life. What does rejection look like for you in this suicide loss grief journey?

"'He will wipe every tear from their eyes.
There will be no more death' or mourning or crying or pain,
for the old order of things has passed away."
~ Revelation 21:4

For God did not send his Son into the world
to condemn the world,
but to save the world through him.
~ John 3:17

145

The LORD is compassionate and gracious,
slow to anger, abounding in love.
He will not always accuse, nor will he harbor his anger forever;
he does not treat us as our sins deserve
or repay us according to our iniquities.
For as high as the heavens are above the earth,
so great is his love for those who fear him;
as far as the east is from the west,
so far has he removed our transgressions from us.
~ Psalm 103:8-12

It feels like suicide is the ultimate rejection. It leads to a feeling that you can never trust anyone or anything. Being rejected leads to distrust. You may have these thoughts:

"Any man I ever love will leave me and reject me."
"Any person I put my trust in will leave me."
"I gave birth to my child; now they have left me."
"She was my best friend; why did she leave me to do life without her?"
"My mom, my rock, is gone – so was I not good enough as a child?"

Unfortunately, rejection causes isolation, feelings of abandonment, and loneliness. You feel your loved one did this intentionally to you. Even though there were other family members or friends in your loved one's life, you still take it as a personal rejection – just as each of those other people also feels personally rejected because of this death by suicide. You are now left alone to take care of what is left behind, from the feelings to the bills to be paid. You feel abandoned.

The loneliness comes from being alone after others have rejected you due to the death being a suicide. You feel rejected because of the judgment passed. You feel left out and isolated in your feelings, as no one else understands where you are emotionally.

Or you feel isolated because you are no longer part of a couple. You feel like you are no longer a parent, since your only child is gone. You feel alone because you no longer have your BFF (Best Friend Forever). You feel like an orphan because your only living parent is now gone.

Total Disconnection. From All People, From All Things.

Rejected.

In reality, the suicide had nothing to do with you. Your loved one was not selfish. Your loved one felt they were doing you a favor by ending their life, as they were consumed by the feeling that they were a burden. Based on where they were in their thoughts, they were being selfless, not selfish. We know they were not a burden. We must remind ourselves: our loved one was not rational when they made the decision to take their life.

I felt like I was rejected in the worst kind of way. My mind told me that my boyfriend taking his life was not personal towards me, but my heart felt differently. We didn't break up. It's not like we were married and then got a divorce. Having no closure feels like rejection. He had the final say. I didn't even get to say good-bye.

I finally realized that he didn't leave me; it was just too painful for him to stay. He wasn't rejecting me at all. It wasn't about me at all.

Your child wasn't telling you that you failed them as a parent. Your best friend wasn't telling you that you were not a good friend. Your parent wasn't telling you that you didn't make them proud. Your sister or brother wasn't saying that they didn't want to be your sibling. Your partner wasn't telling you that you were not a good spouse or girlfriend/boyfriend. It was not personal towards you. Your child, best friend, partner, sibling, or loved one wasn't rejecting you. They just couldn't take their pain any longer.

REGRET

noun – a feeling of sadness, repentance, or disappointment over something that has happened or been done (Lexico.com)

verb – feel sad, repentant, or disappointed over (something that has happened or been done, especially a loss or missed opportunity) (Lexico.com)

In any death, there is regret. With the shock, blame, stigma, and questions surrounding you after the suicide, there seems to be an overload of *"I should have . . ."* – *"I could have . . ."* – *"I would have . . ."* thoughts or words. The feeling of regret is deeper and more intense with suicide loss.

My last communications with my boyfriend were via text messages. I wish I could have heard his voice one more time, even if we were not getting along right before he ended his life.

You may regret that you didn't get to say goodbye.
"If only I could have hugged her and said goodbye."

You may regret that you didn't get to say *"I love you"* one more time.

You may regret things said in an argument before they died.
"I told her I wished she was dead and that I didn't care. I so regret using those words and not having better control of my words in anger. I didn't mean what I said."

You may realize that you regret taking the time you spent with your loved one for granted.
"I didn't sit and listen to him during our normally planned morning time together. I sped out of the house, late for work, again."
"I thought we always had tomorrow."
"I wish I had told her thank you for making my lunch that day."

You may regret that you didn't do things differently with or for your loved one.

"I should have insisted that she let me take her to rehab."

You may regret not seeing the signs or getting the hints that were left by your loved one.

"I thought he was being thoughtful by giving his baseball card collection to his best friend. I didn't know that was a sign."

Unfortunately, regret often leads to guilt. And guilt is not good for our healing.

If we could change the perspective just a little, the regrets may not sting so much. Try to turn regret around and make it a positive. Live each day intentionally and with purpose. Keep a grateful heart, and verbalize it to others. Laugh often. Forgive, even when not asked to. Complain less. Love others.

Instead of regretting the moments you'll no longer have with your loved one, savor the moments you had. Turn the regret around to gratitude.

I thank my God every time I remember you.
~ Philippians 1:3

I have not stopped giving thanks for you,
remembering you in my prayers.
~ Ephesians 1:16

Brothers and sisters,
I do not consider myself yet to have taken hold of it.
But one thing I do: forgetting what is behind
and straining toward what is ahead . . .
~ Philippians 3:13

149

He has made everything beautiful in its time.
He has also set eternity in the human heart;
yet no one can fathom what God has done
from beginning to end.
~ Ecclesiastes 3:11

And the God of all grace,
who called you to his eternal glory in Christ,
after you have suffered a little while,
will himself restore you
and make you strong, firm and steadfast.
To him be the power for ever and ever. Amen.
~ 1 Peter 5:10-11

Jesus replied,
"No one who puts a hand to the plow and looks back
is fit for service in the kingdom of God."
~ Luke 9:62

On the positive side, regret shows how much life is left inside of us. Eventually, regret awakens us to love in the here and now. We learn to live in the moment and cherish the moment. We start making sure we do everything we can so we won't have regrets in the future when it comes to the people and things we care about. Regret can bring about positive change in us.

RELIEF

noun – a feeling of reassurance and relaxation following release from anxiety or distress (Lexico.com)

. . . if this is so, then the Lord knows how to rescue the godly
from trials and to hold the unrighteous for punishment
on the day of judgment.
~ 2 Peter 2:9

You have searched me, LORD, and you know me.
You know when I sit and when I rise;
you perceive my thoughts from afar.
You discern my going out and my lying down;
you are familiar with all my ways.
Before a word is on my tongue
you, LORD, know it completely.
You hem me in behind and before,
and you lay your hand upon me.
Such knowledge is too wonderful for me,
too lofty for me to attain.
Where can I go from your Spirit?
Where can I flee from your presence?
If I go up to the heavens, you are there;
if I make my bed in the depths, you are there.
If I rise on the wings of the dawn,
if I settle on the far side of the sea,
even there your hand will guide me,
your right hand will hold me fast.
If I say, "Surely the darkness will hide me
and the light become night around me,"
even the darkness will not be dark to you;
the night will shine like the day,
for darkness is as light to you.
For you created my inmost being;
you knit me together in my mother's womb.
I praise you because I am fearfully and wonderfully made;
your works are wonderful, I know that full well.
My frame was not hidden from you
when I was made in the secret place,
when I was woven together in the depths of the earth.
Your eyes saw my unformed body;
all the days ordained for me were written in your book
before one of them came to be.
How precious to me are your thoughts, God!
How vast is the sum of them!

Were I to count them,
they would outnumber the grains of sand—
when I awake, I am still with you.
If only you, God, would slay the wicked!
Away from me, you who are bloodthirsty!
They speak of you with evil intent;
your adversaries misuse your name.
*Do I not hate those who hate you, L*ORD*,*
and abhor those who are in rebellion against you?
I have nothing but hatred for them;
I count them my enemies.
Search me, God, and know my heart;
test me and know my anxious thoughts.
See if there is any offensive way in me,
and lead me in the way everlasting.
~ Psalm 139

As much as I hate to admit it, I was relieved that I didn't have to stay in constant 24-hour misery worrying about my boyfriend any longer. I didn't have to worry about getting a call that he had wrecked his car, was in jail or was dead.

"I didn't have to worry that she was locked up in jail for a DUI."
"I didn't have to give her more money to satisfy her habit."
"I didn't have to give the family excuses when she didn't show up
*   – again."*

Our loved one may have caused our lives to be painful before the suicide. We may have lived in fear, afraid that they were going to kill themselves, spend too much money shopping, do drugs, or go on a drinking binge. Maybe you are relieved that you won't get another call that your loved one had overdosed again.

"Is that the creditor calling again?"
"He almost died six months ago when he took a half of a bottle of
*   aspirin with a half bottle of Jack Daniels."*

There may have been verbal or even physical abuse because of our loved one.

"If she threw something at me in the house one more time, I am not sure what I would have done."

We may feel relieved that we no longer have to deal with the anxiety of our loved one's issues. You may have had to deal with your loved one borrowing money and not paying it back. Or your loved one may have stayed away for days at a time, without you knowing if they would come home alive. You may have been afraid that they were in jail again. Or you may have been fearful that this time they were in rehab – again – wouldn't help with their addiction. You may have had mixed emotions frequently, knowing something was wrong that they weren't communicating. Your daily life may have been interrupted time and time again with their drama.

When they took their life, the destructive behavior ended, which gives us relief. We are relieved they are gone because we had been putting up with demands from our loved one. We had been dealing with a troubled personality, which was disruptive to our lives and an obstruction to our peace of mind. It was exhausting and detrimental to our wellbeing to deal with our loved one's depression, suicidal threats, and irrational behaviors that always kept us off balance. Their issues created an environment without peace for us.

Feeling relieved is normal and a true feeling in suicide loss grief. You don't have to feel ashamed because you feel relieved.

Still, feeling relief that our loved one is gone does create guilt. We feel guilty for being relieved that we don't have to bail them out of jail, pick up their slack, or drop them off at rehab – again. How can we reconcile the guilt with the relief?

Suffering and grief are different experiences.
Suffering is re-living pain. Grief is relieving the pain.
~ Dr. Shawne Duperon

Even in the situation of a terminally ill person, the caregiver in the family will feel relieved when their loved one passes away. The terminally ill loved one's pain is over. Also, the sleepless nights, stress, caring for the person 24 hours a day, and running to doctor's appointments are all over for the caregiver. It's not that the caregiver didn't want to do these things for their loved one; it just takes a toll mentally, physically, and emotionally. Don't feel guilty because of your relief. It is normal to feel relieved.

We may also feel guilty about our relief that our loved one is now out of anguish and pain and is no longer suffering. We would be relieved if our loved one who had been suffering from a terminal illness like cancer – couldn't eat, barely breathing, and was a rack of bones – finally passed away. They passed away: they are in no more pain.

So, why do we feel guilty when our loved one who was in mental pain and suffering beyond our understanding took their life to end the pain?

As much as I don't understand what my boyfriend was going through – a mental hell on earth – I wouldn't bring him back. Why would I want him back here in so much pain? I loved him enough to push my personal pain and sorrow aside to be compassionate towards his pain, even though I could not understand. I must accept his irrational behavior that ended his life.

Accepting and agreeing are not the same. If we see someone we love suffering physically through cancer or a breathing disorder, we are sad that they are suffering, and we don't want them to suffer. With suicide, we can't always see what our loved one was experiencing, which makes it harder for us to understand the depth of their pain. But not one of us would want our loved one to suffer. I don't agree with his decision, but I have to have compassion towards the pain and what led him to take his life.

It is a never-ending roller coaster to have a loved one who is terminally ill, mentally ill, addicted, or abusive. So, when that loved one passes away, it is a relief to not be on that emotional, physical, and verbal roller coaster any longer. It's okay to feel relieved. And it's okay to express that. People who don't understand may look at you weirdly when you express the relief, but that is okay. Don't let what others think get in the way of you expressing your feelings during this grief journey.

HOMEWORK

1 – How do you feel rejected, and by whom? Have you rejected someone during this journey? Whom, and why? How can you make amends?

2 – Do you have regrets about something you did or didn't do or say? How can you turn that regret around for good?

3 – Did your loved one stress you out and cause you great anxiety? Journal about those experiences. Writing will help release those feelings.

4 – Are you relieved that your loved one is gone? How? And how do you feel about the feeling of relief?

5 – How can you turn rejection, regret, and relief around for good?

Practical Encouragement

Which Bible verse would help you get through the feelings of rejection, regret, and conflicted relief? Write it down and leave it somewhere you will see it often – on the bathroom mirror, on the fridge, on the coffee maker, on your phone. Try to memorize it and repeat it to yourself when those feelings come up.

Is there something you want to do that will cause you regret if you don't do it? Plan to go do that thing!

WEEK 13

Love and Grace
Forgiveness
Joy and Happiness

You will feel love again. Grace is an act of love and is possible in suicide loss. We will experience forgiveness. Yes, joy does come in the morning. It is hard to believe, but you will be happy again. You will laugh. You will have joy. Don't give up. God gives us hope.

> *"For I know the plans I have for you," declares the* L*ORD,*
> *"plans to prosper you and not to harm you,*
> *plans to give you hope and a future."*
> ~ Jeremiah 29:11

Enjoying life again will feel foreign and strange. You may even feel guilty for enjoying life, especially in living life without your loved one. But you will feel love again. You will love others again. And you will feel the love of others. You will feel grace and give grace. You will show forgiveness and receive forgiveness. You will experience joy and happiness again. You will also play a part in the joy and happiness of others. Don't give up hope. In time, the healing gives way to the positive.

LOVE and GRACE

LOVE
noun – a profoundly tender, passionate affection for another person. a feeling of warm personal attachment or deep affection, as for a parent, child, or friend (Dictionary.com)

verb – to hold dear, cherish; to feel a lover's passion, devotion, or tenderness for (Merriam-Webster Dictionary)

GRACE

noun – courteous goodwill; (in Christian belief) the free and unmerited favor of God, as manifested in the salvation of sinners and the bestowal of blessings (Lexico.com)

verb – bring honor or credit to (someone or something) by one's attendance or participation (Lexico.com)

Show grace to yourself. You are not perfect. *"Should have done more, said more, loved more . . ."* Maybe the relationship wasn't all it could have been between you and your loved one, but you can still be thankful for what it was. It will be hard, but you may need to show grace to others also.

What is expressing grace? Instead of responding with a harsh word when there has been an offense, just remain quiet and say nothing. Be gentle with words to others and in how you talk to yourself. Ask for forgiveness and/or forgive others (and yourself) with kind words and actions. Show your gratitude. Cover your actions and words in love. That is what grace is.

Love. Just because your loved one is not in front of you on this earth doesn't mean your love for them stops, lessens, or ends. Your love is now mixed in with the grief of loss and of missing them. I have realized that, the harder you love someone, the greater the depth of grief when they are no longer with you.

The sum of our experiences (good and bad) develops our character. It brings us to who we are. My momma always said, *"It builds character to do things you don't want to do."* Well, I never thought I would ever understand the grief of suicide loss or the pain that comes with this unique grief. I feel I have gained lots of character. *"I've got enough now, Lord. Thanks anyway, but I thought I had enough character and didn't need this suicide loss grief journey."* But I must keep Pushing Through. Pushing Through this life-changing event has increased my character. My prayer is to glorify God in my pain, and to help others.

Circumstances of life don't make you – they reveal you! What do I become because of this experience of suicide loss grief? I am stronger than I thought I was. I have loved in ways I didn't know I could. I have a whole new level of compassion for others. My heart aches for those who suffer from mental illness – something I can't see with my eyes.

No person can replace another, but you can reinvest your love to others. No matter how much love we give away to others, we can never run out. Love is not something that ends – just as God loves: He never runs out of love for us.

For God so loved the world,
that he gave his only begotten Son,
that whosoever believeth in him should not perish,
but have everlasting life.
~ John 3:16 (KJV)

For God loved the world in this way:
He gave his one and only Son,
so that everyone who believes in him will not perish
but have eternal life.
~ John 3:16 (HCSB – Holman Christian Standard Bible)

God giving the world His son. THAT is love. We loved our loved one so deeply. They loved us. Imagine that God's love for you is greater than all the love between you and your loved one. Just – wow!

We must allow good in our life. You have to let yourself be loved. It's a decision. It's scary to be vulnerable. Love will come from co-workers, friends, neighbors, relatives, church family, friends of friends, school friends, and even strangers. This may be an area where you may need to take baby steps. Being vulnerable allows trust. In the aftermath of a suicide, trust is not automatic. Be patient with learning to trust. Ask God for discernment about trusting others, so you don't let the wrong people into your circle to love.

Let the pride go: ask for help when you need it. And let others love on you when you have a need. Love is an action word, not a feeling. It's okay to ask for help. It's okay to let your neighbor cut your grass for you. It's okay to ask your best friend to drive you to a doctor's appointment because you are scared to go alone.

Live the life your loved one would have wanted you to live, full of grace for yourself and others. And love – always love.

FORGIVENESS

noun – letting go of past grudges or lingering anger against a person or persons (Yourdictionary.com)
SYNONYMS
pardon, absolution, exoneration, dispensation, indulgence, understanding, tolerance, purgation, clemency, mercy, pity, lenience (Lexico.com)

Forgiveness is a hard process in suicide loss grief. Processes take time. Forgiveness is not an emotion. It isn't an automatic event.

Just how are we supposed to forgive? I don't think I was mentally able to even think about the forgiving process until about 60 days after my boyfriend's death.

"For if you forgive other people when they sin against you,
your heavenly Father will also forgive you.
But if you do not forgive others their sins,
your Father will not forgive your sins."
~ Matthew 6:14-15

Forgiveness is the act of surrender. You surrender your human feelings of judgment to God. God is truly the only one in the position to judge. When we surrender the feeling of judgment, it is then that we forgive. God wants us to forgive ourselves and others.

First you need to forgive yourself. WOW! This takes time. This takes patience. This takes a lot of mental processing. It will take the whole grieving process to work through forgiving yourself.

Second, we need to forgive our loved one for taking their life. This will be a process as well. Forgiving them does not mean you forget them. Forgiving them releases us from so much heaviness in our hearts.

Forgiving the world that caused the pain of our loved one and forgiving our loved one for taking their life are two different things. Which of these two should we do? Which is more important? We need to do both. I hate suicide. I need to forgive the pain from the world that engulfed my boyfriend. But can I really do that? Getting to the root of his pain isn't so easy. So it is easier to forgive my boyfriend. THAT pain he felt left him at his last breath, and I believe it jumped on me. As I Push Through this journey, THAT pain will ease up, and as it does, I will forgive THAT pain and the world that caused it.

We feel burdened and bad about the things we said or did to our loved one. We never got a chance to make things right and apologize or seek forgiveness. Ask God for this forgiveness. Ask

God to clear the guilt you carry for unforgiveness. No, we can't directly ask our loved one for forgiveness, and they can't ask us to forgive them. But God can be the One to carry the burden of our and our loved one's forgiveness. Ask Him to forgive you in the place of that person.

Forgive others – family and friends – for things that were said or not said, and things that were done or not done. Most people are morally torn on the topic of suicide, and they may not reach out or be there for you in your grief as you had expected them to. Be purposeful to forgive them. Pray that God will fill your life with people who understand what you are going through – either people who personally understand your grief due to suicide loss, or people who are just willing to try to understand your journey.

There was a time when I had to show forgiveness to my family. The first Christmas without my boyfriend, my family did not even mention his name at our family gathering. All I could think was: *Dang, last Christmas, we were all laughing, playing games, eating, and celebrating the day. Now, my family acts as if he didn't even exist.* I was so hurt. I was trying to understand that they probably didn't know if they should mention his name or not, but I was still hurt – even though there was no intention of hurt on their part. I had to take the high road and forgive them.

To truly forgive, we need to forget. This doesn't mean we forget our loved one, but we forget the pain associated with the suicide. This is not automatic. Be patient with the process.

People think forgiveness is an emotion, but it's not; it's an active decision. It is not automatic. It takes time and effort. It's a process. God can help us in this process, so ask Him to help you forgive.

This verse rings in my thoughts often. This Bible verse shows that forgiving someone is not an emotion but a process.

Then Peter came to Jesus and asked,
"Lord, how many times shall I forgive my brother or sister
who sins against me? Up to seven times?"
Jesus answered, "I tell you, not seven times,
but seventy-seven times*.
~ Matthew 18:21-22
(*Footnote: Matthew 18:22 Or *seventy times seven*)

We are to forgive over and over and over.

And over.

Withholding forgiveness is dangerous to your health and hinders the "moving forward" process in suicide loss grief. In unforgiveness, we build up resentment. Resentment seems to just grow, like a fungus. It will sap your strength and drain your heart of goodness. Unforgiveness becomes a weight to your soul.

Unforgiveness is like drinking poison yourself
and waiting for the other person to die.
~ Marianne Williamson

During this suicide loss grief process, we may actually be the one who needs to ask for forgiveness. There will be times when you say or do things that are not typical of your normal behavior. And, due to this grief process, you may not even realize you hurt someone until much later, after the offense. Once you realize the offense, ask for forgiveness. Be good to yourself about this and just make it right when you realize the wrong. Acknowledge it, apologize, and ask for forgiveness. Then let it go. We cannot control if someone forgives us. That is on them. We can only do our part.

JOY and HAPPINESS

JOY

noun – the emotion evoked by well-being, success, or good fortune or by the prospect of possessing what one desires; the expression or exhibition of such emotion; a state of happiness or felicity, a source or cause of delight (Merriam-Webster Dictionary)

verb – to experience great pleasure or delight (Merriam-Webster Dictionary)

> *A cheerful heart is good medicine . . .*
> ~ Proverbs 17:22a

Joy is a feeling of great pleasure and happiness. Joy is finding peace, hope, and purpose in any circumstances, no matter how difficult. Joy is coming out of pain with a new outlook, new meaning, and a new purpose in life. Joy is also an action. Joy is possible with this suicide loss grief.

Happiness and joy are different. Happiness is an emotion. In happiness, we have feelings of contentment, satisfaction, bliss, and intense pleasure. Happiness is externally triggered. Happiness is based on other people, things, places, thoughts, and events. Joy is stronger, yet less common, than happiness. Joy is internal. Joy is consistent. Joy comes from the Lord. Joy comes in freedom and peace from within.

What can you do now to receive the joy the Lord has for you? What about happiness? How can you find "a cheerful heart" right now, where you are in your grief?

The place to be happy is here, the time to be happy is now. The way to be happy is to help make others happy. GO! Pushing Through will generate happiness.

There are so many ways we can help others. Get creative. Go help others in an area that you enjoy.

Do you like animals? Go volunteer at an animal shelter.

What about gardening? You see your elderly neighbor has weeds in her flower beds. Go clean them out for her.

Or your friend needs the oil changed in his truck, but he can't do it himself as he normally does, because he had surgery recently. You like to tinker on vehicles. Go change the oil and filter in his truck for him.

Joy and light, praise and laughter – they are on their way. Be ready for it. Anticipate it.

Push Through.

One day, you will get to the point when you rejoice that your loved one is no longer in their pain on this earth. One day, you will rejoice that you had the love you had with your loved one. One day, you will rejoice as you realize that this journey of suicide loss grief brings good, and that there is healing.

Before you speak, listen
Before you write, think
Before you spend, earn
Before you invest, investigate
Before you criticize, wait
Before you pray, forgive
Before you quit, try
Before you retire, save
Before you die, give
~ William Arthur Ward

I will exalt you, LORD, for you lifted me out of the depths
and did not let my enemies gloat over me.
LORD my God, I called to you for help, and you healed me.
You, LORD, brought me up from the realm of the dead;
you spared me from going down to the pit.
Sing the praises of the LORD, you his faithful people;
praise his holy name.
For his anger lasts only a moment,
but his favor lasts a lifetime;
weeping may stay for the night,
but rejoicing comes in the morning.
~ Psalm 30:1-5

HOMEWORK

1 – Has anyone shown grace to you? Have you shown anyone grace? Write down what this looks like for you and how giving and getting grace are different.

2 – What does love mean to you? To whom do you need to show love? Why? When you are ready, reach out to those people.

3 – Is your heart open to love, or have you put a wall up to protect yourself? Journal about this.

4 – Whom do you need to forgive? Write letters to those people, even if you never send them. Journal your feelings.

5 – Have you felt joy yet? Have you been happy or expressed happiness? Journal about those moments. What memories do you have of moments with your loved one that were happy or joyful? Put the memories on paper and go back over these moments to bring a smile to your heart.

Practical Encouragement

Make a list of all of the positive qualities of your loved one. Let the memories bring you joy.

Go out and express love to one person, a group, or an organization. Journal about the experience.

WEEK 14

Stigma
Secondary Wounds

In the grieving of a suicide loss, we are surrounded by stigmas. The stigmas are wrapped up in accusations. We have lost our loved one, the greatest wound to our life. We also have wounds that are secondary losses to the loss of our loved one.

STIGMA

noun – a mark of disgrace associated with a particular circumstance, quality, or person (Momentumformentalhealth.org)

I have been trying to understand why the word "suicide" puts people on edge. Why isn't it easily discussed? Why is it a taboo topic? These may be questions that I never get answers to. Suicide is a focus of controversy and outrage. Suicide is a political, moral, and religious hot topic with varied beliefs and understandings. But why?

Why is suicide not openly discussed, like someone's death would be if they had died from a car accident? Why do people want to hide the truth of suicide? Is it because we don't know the reasons they took their life? We don't know the truths of suicide. And most of the questions we ask in suicide loss grief never get answers. We will never know the complete truth. Maybe most people have come to realize they will not have the answers to the questions, so they don't want to talk about it.

It really bothers me when the words *"committed suicide"* are used. People commit adultery or murder, or they are committed to institutions. *"Committed suicide"* is so negative. We say someone *"died by cancer"* or *"died by car accident"*, so we should say *"died by suicide."* I have also heard *"died by mental illness"* and *"died as a result of PTSD."*

I try to gently suggest to people who use the term *"committed suicide"* that my loved one died by suicide or died due to the pains of PTSD. I try to explain how negative *"committed suicide"* is – that this grief due to suicide loss is so painful, and that I don't need additional pain from hearing the words *"committed suicide."* These two words cause great pain to those suffering a suicide loss. We feel as if another arrow is being shot our way – another sign of the stigma surrounding suicide.

Society tends to look at families differently after a suicide death – like they are unclean or crazy, or like something is "wrong" with the family. Some may think that the idea of suicide is "catching", like catching a cold. I wish I could tell people: if someone is around me, they are not going to feel like they are suicidal. I am not a contagious germ just because my loved one took their life. Others may feel they will fall "prey" to suicide if they are around me, because my loved one died by suicide. Suicide causes so much division.

Suicide goes against the natural order of life. Society views suicide as an ending that can't be discussed or mentioned. It seems that society wants to ignore suicide – both the word itself, and the people who are left behind after suffering a loss due to suicide. Really, society "pretends" to ignore suicide, but it is actually full of whispering and questioning and blaming. Suicide is wrapped up in accusations and question marks.

There was a young man from church who died. He was found in his apartment. There was no note. There was no obvious reason for the death. He was in his early 40s, seemingly physically healthy. Everyone knew he had suffered from some depression and PTSD. So, it amused me that everyone was questioning and whispering, *"Did he kill himself?" "Was there a note?" "Has the medical examiner's report been released?" "I was just hanging out with him and I didn't notice any signs."* Everyone seemed obsessed with knowing if he died by suicide. It just baffled me. I can't understand the fascination with people wanting the details or wondering if it was a suicide or not.

Come to find out, he died from a heart condition. To me, it was simple: he was gone. It didn't matter why or how he died; he was not here any longer to be my friend. I was sad. But to others, the method of death was of great importance. I don't get it.

In society, the fact that your loved one died is lost. Instead, the focus is on HOW your loved one died. Why is this so important to people? We don't focus on someone dying from old age or a car accident, needing every detail. *Did they leave a note? What method did they use to take their life? Did you see the signs?* Then the stigma starts. *Why does it matter how my loved one died?* THAT is the million-dollar question. And here we are, once again, with the unanswered and endless questions.

If you deny to others that the death was suicide, you end up trapped in lies and confusion. It will make recovery and healing longer than it should be if you can't be honest about the way your loved one's life ended. It's okay to be honest and transparent, even if it is scary to be transparent and to trust. It takes time to be comfortable with being transparent, so be patient with yourself.

I am still trying to understand why people avoid the subject of suicide. If my boyfriend had died while defending the freedoms of our country, there would have been a parade celebrating his life. He would be a hero. But, because he died from the wounds of life, his existence is ignored. He suffered from PTSD, but no one wants to acknowledge that. He didn't get a parade. No one wanted to acknowledge that his cause of death was suicide as a result of mental illness.

Because our loved one's death was a result of suicide, others blame and avoid. You feel people look at you with judgment. You feel shamed by others. You feel accused of wrongdoing. Rarely does society understand how to offer support in suicide grief. It is easier to avoid and blame than to understand suicide loss grief.

We get shunned by society as if the suicide was our fault. It's almost like we can hear people saying:

"Why didn't you stop him from taking his life?"
"What did you do to cause him to want to take his life?"
"Did you see the signs?"
"Did he leave a note?"
"Did you know she was suicidal?"
"What caused it – did y'all get into a fight?"
"Why did she do it?"
"Had she tried it before?"

NO ONE is to blame for a suicide. The person took their own life. It was their lone decision. The person who died by suicide is the only person to blame. But we won't blame our loved one who took their own life. Others won't blame our loved one. We want to blame it on someone or something. But there is no one reason why someone takes their own life. We cannot get wrapped up in the blame game.

The blaming and avoidance reinforce guilt and self-blame, exacerbate isolation, and make it difficult to talk about our feelings. Guilt, blame, isolation, and silence seem to be magnified in suicide loss grief, which makes the healing process so hard. These are all speed bumps on the journey.

We may get snubbed at work, at church, by neighbors, and by friends and family. Being snubbed is hard to understand or receive. Losing our loved one has been hard enough. Then to hear negative words about suicide – or to have others not want to talk about the suicide – makes it extremely difficult. Really hard. I would see people at church walking towards me, then turn away or look elsewhere when they saw me coming. Friends would talk to me, but with no mention of my boyfriend. A friend I used to have dinner with weekly stopped asking me to go to dinner. Disconnection and isolation.

In our suicide loss grief, we feel isolated and alone. We can't seem to find others to grieve with us. All we want is someone to journey with us – someone who will understand where we are and why.

After my boyfriend's death, I had no one around me who loved him like I did – no one who could grieve with me. My boyfriend's family lived out of state, and they made it clear they wanted nothing to do with me after his death. We had been close, so it was even more hurtful when they disowned me after my boyfriend's death. So, I felt very alone in my grief. More questions. *Why couldn't I grieve with them? What had I done?*

But, even if you have family around you, you can still feel alone in this journey. Maybe others who loved and cared about your loved one are not taking the same path you are in this journey. It's okay: no two people grieve the same. It's normal to feel alone.

In suicide grief, you get less support. For example, when my momma died from cancer, people showed up with casseroles, meals, flowers, and cards. The offers of support were endless. People asked, even months later, how I was doing. With my boyfriend: no meals, three cards, two flower arrangements, and one gardenia bush. I am grateful for those who reached out to me, but I couldn't help thinking: *death is death*. Gone is gone. Both my momma and my boyfriend were gone. My heart ached for both. Yet, the way people dealt with me were like night and day.

Mostly, people don't know what to say in suicide loss grief. I understand that. But I wanted to scream to others, *"Say something!"* Even my sister admitted to not saying anything at Christmas because she didn't want to make me sad by reminding me of my boyfriend. I WANT to be reminded of this man I loved. I miss him terribly! Of course, I am going to be sad. He took his life and is no longer here on this earth. But I do not want to forget him or act like he never existed. My family talks of my momma and her life on this earth. So why not my boyfriend? More questions.

It can be very confusing to understand why others act or don't act as we expect. I have tried to be compassionate and show grace to others. I have tried not to be mad at others for not behaving towards me as I wish they would. And I have learned that it is my responsibility to communicate to others what I expect. They can't read my mind. But I know that I just didn't have it in me immediately after my boyfriend's death to communicate what I needed, wanted, or felt – really, anything.

In this grief journey, we end up thinking, *"I should be able to do this by myself."* We think we are strong and don't need others. We don't open ourselves up to the help of others. This is pride. It is okay to ask for help. We must humble ourselves. It is an easier journey if others come alongside us. We must let others join us if they want to join us.

When pride comes, then comes disgrace,
but with humility comes wisdom.
~ Proverbs 11:2

In his pride the wicked man does not seek him;
in all his thoughts there is no room for God.
~ Psalm 10:4

Suicide is a tangle of guilt, anger, and disbelief with few "safe place" shelters available to repair one's self. Hopefully, if you are reading this, you have found your safe place shelter. We may find ourselves clinging to our safe place shelter and holding onto it with an unrelenting grasp. This may not be healthy. We need to make sure we are healthy in our safe place shelter. We must keep moving forward. Our safe place shelter should allow our moving forward and encourage the Pushing Through. Seek healthy shelters, where growth and healing are nurtured.

For those who want to help you in your journey, tell them what you need. Be specific. The "helper" gets confused, embarrassed, or inhibited because of our silence. Be vocal about what you need and want. If you can't be vocal, write it down. (See the "Catch-22 Cards" section at the end of this chapter for some practical tips about this.) There are a few people in your tribe who will show up for you. Embrace their love and the heart they have for your grief. Let them help you. Let them love on you.

It may help to say to other people: *"Please listen to me. You don't have to have answers – just listen."* Good listening skills lead to good talking. There is healing in talking. We need to say what we are feeling. We are not looking for advice, solutions, or even comforting words. Sometimes we need to tell people that we just want them to listen. It will help in our healing process to let it out, without judgment or advice from the person listening.

How others stayed away, neglected me, ignored me, and did not ask me any questions about how I was or anything about my loved one have made my suicide loss grief a very lonely and confusing process. Sometimes I just wanted to scream, *"My boyfriend is gone. Please let me talk about him!"*

The old me was a very strong and independent person. Immediately after experiencing my boyfriend's suicide, I became a weak, no-voice, no-energy, no-boundaries, lifeless person. I have been Pushing Through, post-loss, and there has been healing, but I am still not who I was before. So much changed. This whole experience made me feel as if I no longer knew what to believe in or who to trust.

People in my life have not known what to do with the "New Me." I didn't even know who I was; how could anyone else know? It took time and patience to know who the New Me was. I had to learn to be the New Me. I am even starting to like the New Me, scars and all.

So, don't beat yourself up for not liking the "New You" at first. And others who want to know the New You will learn who you are. Patience. One day, your light will shine again.

Suicide leaves a feeling of numbness, sadness, and betrayal in those left behind. Even those who care about the you, the suicide loss survivor – though they may not have been close to or even known the suicide victim – will have feelings about the suicide. Most people ask, *"What could I have said to or done for the victim?"*

My tax preparer was around my boyfriend a week before he took his life. Even though she didn't know him, she sensed something was up with him. She later told me that she questioned herself as to whether she should have mentioned her uneasiness to me.

She had attempted suicide herself in her past, and she sensed there was something just not well with him.

A suicidal person is in a black hole of never-ending pain. You can give and give to that person, but you just can't fill up that black hole for them. Only God can fill the void created by the never-ending black hole. It is not our responsibility to fill the black holes of other people. And, as we feel that we are in our own black hole, we must know that God is there for us in this black hole of suicide loss grief – just as He was with our loved one in their pain. God – not me, not you – is the Rescuer.

"Be strong and courageous.
Do not be afraid or terrified because of them,
for the LORD your God goes with you;
he will never leave you nor forsake you."
~ Deuteronomy 31:6

Suicide happened. I am sorry it did. I wouldn't have chosen suicide for my loved one or this suicide loss grief for myself. I pray that I will get to the point when I will feel like it is over. I will feel like I can wash my hands of this grief and the negativity that has come with it. I will have overcome the stigmas society has placed on suicide loss. I will be free. I will know it's time to get on with my life. And it will be because I Pushed Through and Pushed Through, over and over again.

My loved one will always be a part of me. I am not washing my hands of my loved one. But I will be free from the painful parts of the suicide loss grief journey.

God is there for you, as He has been for me. Lean into Him. He does the healing!

And remember, He will leave the 99 to rescue me and you!

"What do you think?
If a man owns a hundred sheep,
and one of them wanders away,
will he not leave the ninety-nine on the hills
and go to look for the one that wandered off?"
~ Matthew 18:12

SECONDARY WOUNDS

It is hard to believe how one decision affects so many lives. *"Each suicide directly affects a minimum of 32 people"*. (SAVE – Suicide Awareness Voices of Education)

Secondary wounds are the products of suicide in addition to the loss of our loved one. Friendships, family relationships, work relationships, community involvement, church relationships, social circles, finances, health, home life, and any other imaginable circumstances are all open to change after suicide loss. And, because of the stigma, shame, guilt, blame, unanswered questions, and taboo nature of suicide, these changes will be different from secondary wounds resulting from other types of death.

What is really hard to understand and accept is that all relationships change. Most family relationships change after suicide loss – and not in a positive way, because of the blame game. People at your job may not be so understanding of your crying or "down" episodes. Your romantic relationship may end. Relationships with friends often trail off to nothing, or they just are not what they used to be.

People at church are different towards you. You may feel judged. I have friends who had to change Sunday school classes at church after their son's death. The relationships with neighbors change as they stare and don't speak like they used to. The social circles change. Relationships with people at school feel different, as you just can't concentrate on school like you did before.

These changes are hard to accept. Suicide has a strange aftershock, and negatively changed relationships are a big part of the secondary wounds.

The secondary wounds are very present in families. Families tend to lose love and respect, and they may grow bitter and angry towards one another due to guilt, shame, silence, and anger. The family unit becomes another victim of the suicide – especially if family members blame other family members.

What does blaming solve? Nothing. Does blaming make us feel better? No. Or do we think that, if we blame someone, we won't feel blame personally? Maybe. Is blaming someone else better than blaming our loved one who died by suicide? Yes. Does blaming our loved one solve any problems or fix any issue? No. There is no place for blame in death. Unfortunately, blame is a common "secondary wound" after loss due to suicide.

Friends often fade into the distance. They may be there initially after the death. But then they are gone. This happens with family members as well. You may have a sister who showed up immediately after your child died by suicide. She ran errands for you – was there to hug you and listen to you. Then, a few weeks after the memorial service, she is gone. The relationship is back to the way it was before – not a close or strong relationship. Then you have another loss. Another wound.

Whether we want to accept it or not, friendships change. Some friendships don't exist any longer, and other friendships get stronger. New friendships are formed. The people we would never have expected to be there for us step up and become very dear to us. We can't fight this change. It just happens. We can't beat ourselves up because of friendships changing or dissolving. We will have new friendships that we will be forever grateful for.

Some relationships that fade away after suicide loss need to fade away. Don't feel guilty if you must remove people from your life because they are not good for you. You may not even realize who needs to be removed until months after the death. Trim the dead branches from your tree of life so you can have new blooms to produce fruit.

"I am the true vine, and my Father is the gardener.
He cuts off every branch in me that bears no fruit,
while every branch that does bear fruit he prunes
so that it will be even more fruitful.
You are already clean
because of the word I have spoken to you.
Remain in me, as I also remain in you.
No branch can bear fruit by itself; it must remain in the vine.
Neither can you bear fruit unless you remain in me.
I am the vine; you are the branches.
If you remain in me and I in you, you will bear much fruit;
apart from me you can do nothing.
If you do not remain in me,
you are like a branch that is thrown away and withers;
such branches are picked up, thrown into the fire and burned.
If you remain in me and my words remain in you,
ask whatever you wish, and it will be done for you.
This is to my Father's glory, that you bear much fruit,
showing yourselves to be my disciples."
~ John 15:1-8

Your loved one's death affects your dreams – more secondary wounds. You must give up the dream of all the tomorrows with your loved one you won't get to live. Your spouse won't be at the hospital with you when the new grandbaby is born. You won't get to see your daughter graduate from high school. No more shared moments of laughter with your dad. You and your best friend won't be double-dating again. Them being gone is a void that can't be satisfied.

You are no longer a couple. You have one less sibling. Your best friend is gone. You now have one less child to parent. Your spouse is not there beside you in bed at night. A family member won't be at the family get-togethers. Your co-worker is not there to do their job. Your grandchild is gone. Your neighbor isn't at the block party. Your girlfriend is gone. The fiancé is gone, and the wedding had to be canceled. A piece in your puzzle of life is gone. And the void is almost unbearable at times.

Disconnection and isolation are secondary wounds of suicide loss. We feel disconnected from our old self and isolated from the life we knew before the suicide. My life is forever changed. Life as I knew it no longer exists. My loved one died. So did the life I had with my loved one.

Suicide causes an overwhelming and tremendous sense of confusion, displacement, uncertainty, and ambiguity. The future is a little more unknown with your loved one gone. *"Who am I?"* *"Who am I without my loved one?"* More questions. More secondary wounds.

Grief creates wounds. Wounds create scars. Scars need to heal. Scars can be ugly. Scars need love, too. I long to have others love my scars, not just the "pretty" and happy parts of me. It's a joint package of the good and the scars. And it all needs love, not division.

We have to accept that our lives will never be the same. It will be different. It is your goal to heal and Push Through. We must accept the secondary wounds that will also be present in this grief journey. All wounds heal.

"'But I will restore you to health and heal your wounds,'
declares the LORD,
'because you are called an outcast,
Zion for whom no one cares.'"
~ Jeremiah 30:17

HOMEWORK

1 – What stigmas have you experienced? Do you feel you have had to hide the method of death of your loved one?

2 – What would you do/say if you weren't afraid to talk or share or be vulnerable?

3 – What relationships have you seen change the most? Have you had to trim "dead branches"? How did it make you feel?

4 – Name three secondary wounds you have experienced. Journal about them.

5 – How has God helped in the secondary wounds?

Practical Encouragement

Make a list to give to your "safe people" of what you need AND want from them. Give them the list. Talk about it. Practice being open and honest. Practice accepting help.

CATCH-22 CARDS

I came up with the idea of doing communication cards, "Catch-22 Cards", when I realized that it was my responsibility to express to others what I needed or wanted from them. Others cannot read my mind or my heart.

According to Wikipedia, *"A catch-22 is a paradoxical situation from which an individual cannot escape because of contradictory rules or limitations. The term was coined by Joseph Heller, who used it in his 1961 novel* Catch-22.*"*

This applies to our suicide loss grief because we can't escape the paradox: there is healing in talking, but we don't know what to say. We need help from others, but we don't always know how to express it. Since I can't escape my grief or walk away from it, it is my responsibility to communicate with others what I need and want to help me Push Through.

I also like the number 22, since it references the VA's 2012 Suicide Data Report statistic about 22 veteran suicides happening every day in the US. After this report was released, the slogan "22 A DAY" was born. My boyfriend was a veteran, so I have a special place in my heart for our veterans and their suicidal struggles.

And that is why I call these communication cards "Catch-22 Cards."

I believe people do have good intentions and want to help, but all the questions and inquiries about our grief situation can seem overwhelming at times. These cards could help you express what is in your heart when you can't find a way – or don't have the strength – to say it.

Take a stack of index cards and write out simple one-liners of expression. The following are examples:

I do not feel like talking about _____ (your loved one's name in the blank) today.

I do want to talk about _____ today.

I need someone to just listen, not give advice. Will you do that for me?

Since you asked, can you please pray for me in the following ways: _____, _____. Thank you.

I need to run and errand and don't want to go alone. Can you go with me?

If we talk about _____, can we just talk about the happy times?

Today is not a good day for me. I hope you will understand.

I am having a great day today. I am open to conversation about

_____.

I need fresh air. Can we go for a walk?

Will you help me write thank you notes to those I want to express gratitude towards?

Can you drive me to an appointment? I do not want to go alone.

Will you make phone calls for me? I just can't do it today.

I need some items from the grocery store. Can you help me with this errand?

I need you to give me a hug.

I am not up to answering questions. I hope you understand.

I do not want to tell the story again. Maybe later.

I do not have the answers to your questions. Sorry.

I am mad.

I am sad.

I am angry at _____.

I want to have a good day today. Can you suggest something I may enjoy?

Can we go for coffee?

Will you go to a grief meeting with me?

Thank you!

I need to be alone right now.
It will help me if I can be in the company of others. I need a
distraction.
Will you help me find a way to honor _____ 's life?
Will you help me clean out _____'s bedroom/closet/home?
How can I help you today?
I appreciate your concern.
I am grateful for your help during this time.
Please pray for me.

Personalize your "Catch-22 Cards" to fit your own thoughts, feelings, needs and wants. Others will appreciate you expressing what it is you need and want. It will also make others feel less awkward and relieve their discomfort about not knowing what to do or say. This will open the pathway of communication, which will alleviate the loneliness and isolation.

Two are better than one,
because they have a good return for their labor:
If either of them falls down,
one can help the other up.
Ecclesiastes 4:9-10a

The "Catch-22 Cards" can be used in any area of distress. For example: someone going through cancer treatment; someone who has had to put their parent in long-term care; someone going through a divorce – whenever there is an issue in life that is emotionally exhausting to share with others, the "Catch-22 Cards" can be a useful tool to relieve you from depleting yourself emotionally, mentally, and physically.

WEEK 15

Pushing Through
Laughter
New Normal
Gratitude

This week we will talk about some positive aspects of our suicide loss grief journey. Yes, there is positive that comes from this hell on earth we have been experiencing. You will laugh again. And you will have a grateful heart.

PUSHING THROUGH

Every step of this suicide loss grief journey has been an effort of Pushing Through. In suicide loss grief, you must Push Through it to get past it. The experience of suicide loss grief will always be a part of you, but it is not all of you. It is not your identity.

Finish each day and be done with it.
Tomorrow is a new day you shall begin in serenity.
~ Ralph Waldo Emerson

Serenity Prayer
God,
Grant me the Serenity to Accept the things I cannot change,
the Courage to Change the things I can,
and the Wisdom to Know the difference.
~ Niebuhr

Don't get stuck in your story. You can have a victim's mentality or a victor's mentality. Victims wallow in their pain. Don't be a victim. Victors find the silver lining. Victors Push Through. Be victorious in this journey!

If you find yourself getting stuck while trying to Push Through in your suicide loss grief, remember this verse:

"Father, if you are willing, take this cup from me;
yet not my will, but yours be done."
~ Luke 22:42

Just surrender to God whatever is keeping you hung up along your journey. Surrender the pain to God so He can turn it around and use it for good.

And we know that in all things
God works for the good of those who love him,
who have been called according to his purpose.
~ Romans 8:28

It may help you to focus on what could be in the present and future, not what was or what might have been in the past. After this journey, you have the option to rebuild your life differently and better. "Rebuild" doesn't mean to move away, but to move on. Allow God to be your firm foundation for the rebuild. Push Through.

You will experience triggers in your journey. They can be negative or positive triggers. Most triggers cannot be helped, like a song on the radio, a picture you run across, a memory that just comes to mind, or someone saying something that takes you back to your loved one. In the grief process, what was once a negative trigger may turn into a positive trigger, in time. A picture that used to bring a tear to your eyes may now make you smile.

In time, you may want to get rid of purposeful triggers, like a shrine you have created to your loved one. The shrine may serve a purpose for a time, but once it becomes a negative trigger, you need to get rid of it in order to Push Through. Or your shrine may never cause a problem for you in creating negative reactions. If it doesn't become a negative trigger, it is okay to keep it around to preserve the memory of your loved one. You get to decide!

You can decide what is healthy and serves in a positive way for your continued healing. Sometimes a gentle word from a caring friend or relative will help you realize you are stuck and may need to remove a trigger or a behavior from your journey. Push Through.

While Pushing Through, keep in mind that you are in an emotional crisis. You are vulnerable, you are weak, and your judgment can be compromised. Have someone to help you out. Find a helpmate – a family member or friend – to guide you and to help you move beyond the emotional crisis. Having that accountability partner and/or helpmate is important as you Push Through. They should be honest yet gentle with you during your "emotional crisis" phase of grief.

Form your team – your anchors, your tribe, your people. I am an ultra-runner. It is a great community of caring and giving runners. In ultra-running, you have a support crew and a crew chief on race day. The crew chief is there to take care of the runner – before the race, all during the race, and after the race. The crew members will show up at different parts of the race to help the runner. Some people will only do a lap or a leg of the race, some will do a few laps or legs of the race, and some will be there for the entire race. Each person has a part in the success of the runner. They are a team, with the runner at the center and the crew chief/crew members supporting.

So, grab your crew chief and crew members. This is your tribe, your anchor, your people, your team. It is okay if some people have a smaller role than others in your life. Each person is important to your recovery and healing! They all have your back and want you to succeed and heal.

Whatever you do, don't take people for granted. Show gratitude to your "crew members," even if it is a simple "Thank you" or a written card of thanks.

It's important to give people the benefit of the doubt during this suicide loss grief journey. Yet, for your own good, you must also set boundaries. If you can help it, try not to allow people on your team who will disappoint you. Actions speak louder than words. If someone has a history of letting you down in the past, rethink their current role in your life. If you let these types of people in, you would most likely feel rejected – again. You would feel you are being punished by the world – again. Emotionally unsafe people must be cut off. Dead branches must be cut from trees if fruitful blooms are desired. You will bloom again, so cut those dead branches away!

Initially, it might be hard to set boundaries. But, as we continue Pushing Through in our journey, it will become easier to set healthy boundaries. Be courageous in doing this. Be strong. Just remember: boundaries can also leave the bad stuff inside the wall. Keep a door in that boundary so you can not only let the good in, but let the bad out.

"Be strong and courageous.
Do not be afraid or terrified because of them,
for the LORD your God goes with you;
he will never leave you nor forsake you."
~ Deuteronomy 31:6

Ever seen someone living/working in a situation that is not good, but they continue in it anyway? These people are miserable. I call it "functional dysfunction." Urban Dictionary defines this as *"a*

194

person who, while able to minimally function in society, hold a job (at varying degrees of success), feed, clothe, & house themselves, still remains a disaster at nearly all other personal & social aspects of life."

I have a little different take on it. People will live in a situation or environment because it's familiar, even though they know a different way would be better or healthier. They stay with what they know.

An example of this would be the life of an abused wife. She knows what to expect in the abusive marriage. She knows it is wrong. She knows life would be better away from her husband. But she stays, because she knows how it will work out every time he hits. The unknown of "a better life" is too scary, so she stays with what she knows. She remains miserable. She remains in an abusive relationship just because she knows the function of the dysfunction.

Try not to get into any situation in your life that can be classified as functional dysfunction. If you find yourself in such a situation, please try to enlist the help of family and friends outside of the situation to help you get away from the functional dysfunction.

> *"What you allow is what will continue."*
> *"You teach people how to treat you."*
> ~ Dr Phil

Choose your battles with people and issues. You will not be 100% emotionally healthy for a good while – maybe a year or longer. You may need your crew chief to help you during this time. The crew chief or accountability partner can see things from the outside and help guide you to safety, if need be.

Try to live in the moment, day by day. Live in the now. Celebrate today! God brought you through to one more day. Start your day with prayers of thanksgiving.

We need to forgive the past and embrace the present. Forget the "What if"s and embrace the "What is."

Your eyes saw my unformed body;
all the days ordained for me were written in your book
before one of them came to be.
~ Psalm 139:16

Invite Jesus into your pain, emptiness, and loneliness. He will invite you into the "now" of His present peace and joy. He is waiting for you to surrender your hurts to Him.

And the peace of God, which transcends all understanding,
will guard your hearts and your minds in Christ Jesus.
~ Philippians 4:7

Don't run away from your journey. Things can only be healed by staying where you are and working things out. Push Through.

LAUGHTER

I have found laughter to be the best medicine for lifting my spirits and mood. There were many days when laughter was not even an option. I was low. I was drowning in emotional pain. I was heavy. I could not even begin to smile, laugh, or think positive thoughts. Even after several years, I still find it hard to find joy and laugh. I often feel guilty when I do. My boyfriend isn't here to get to laugh. He didn't get to see any birthdays past his 35th. It's not fair that I get to laugh and he doesn't. And laughter was something we shared a lot in together.

But I have realized: I am here. And I get to have joy and laughter! I deserve to have happy days, enjoy wonderful moments with friends and family, laugh until my belly aches, and wear a smile on my heart.

Over the years, I have found it refreshing to tell corny – yet funny – jokes to others. I find it fun to make others laugh, even if I am a little goofy in the process. I have a few joke books, and I try to have jokes on hand for others! I find lots to laugh about in *Biggest Riddle Book in the World* by Joseph Rosenbloom and *Joke and Riddle Bonanza* by Michael J. Pelloski.

Q: What do Cowboys in Texas read?
A: Tex books.

Q: Why do bees hum?
A: They don't know the words.

Q: What is a popular perfume?
A: A best smeller.

Yes, corny. But you did chuckle, if just a little.

How do you feel after you laugh? Don't you feel lighter? Doesn't a smile stay on your face after the laugh has ended? Laughter is a healer. Open yourself to life and be fully present to express laughter.

In laughter, there is complete surrender, which leads to an ultimate release. When you laugh, your soul awakens, opening yourself up to positive energy. Laughter is and always will be the best medicine. Life is just better when you are laughing.

I love people who make me laugh.
I honestly think it's the thing I like most, to laugh.
It cures a multitude of ills.
It's probably the most important thing in a person.
~ Audrey Hepburn

A cheerful heart is good medicine,
but a crushed spirit dries up the bones.
~ Proverbs 17:22

For me, when I need a good laugh, I watch the television show *Impractical Jokers*. It always cheers me up, and sometimes I end up with those true belly laughs. Find a television show, a book of jokes, or someone who can make you laugh when you need a "pick me up."

Be good to yourself. Opening your soul through laughter is being good to yourself. You deserve to laugh, smile, have joy, and live a life of happiness.

NEW NORMAL

He has made everything beautiful in its time.
He has also set eternity in the human heart . . .
~ Ecclesiastes 3:11

I have struggled with my "New Me." I was happy with who I was before the suicide of my boyfriend. And even though I wasn't in need of change or a "New Normal," I got one. I have had to accept this New Me. I don't even know who she is. But she is there.

It was harder for me to accept that I was changed by my grief and trauma than it was for me to (eventually) accept the New Me. Take it easy on yourself. Be good to yourself. Be patient.

You will have to accept that you are changed forever. This may be hard to do, but necessary for moving forward. For me, I just wanted to get off the merry-go-round of crazy grief and return to normalcy. I soon realized my old normal would not return. We are changed – but, while we are picking up the pieces left behind, we get the opportunity to rebuild. We must make our New Normal. We have the freedom to set what our New Normal looks like for us. Let the adventure begin!

No one can define your New Normal but you. Once you have accepted this and your perspective starts to change, you may realize that this New You and New Normal are refreshing and exciting. Possibilities become endless. This New You gets to decide. You set the boundaries. A new chapter in your book is beginning, and you are the author who gets to write that chapter however you want to. That is liberating.

We must decide that what breaks our heart does not destroy our life. We will Push Through this. Remember how you felt when the first love of your life was no longer the love of your life? That moment was horrible. Tears never ended; stomachaches; couldn't eat; couldn't sleep . . . but, in time, the pain dulled. You were not destroyed by that first love ending. It sure did feel like it at first, but time is gracious. You Push Through.

Even in darkness, it is possible to create light.
~ Eli Wiesel

We may be fragile, but we will bounce back. We just won't bounce back to the exact place we were before. But we will bounce back. That is good to know, huh?

You may not feel it right now, but in this suicide loss grief, you have a purpose. You had a purpose before the death of your loved one. And you will continue to have one. It will be different than it was before. Be okay with this new purpose once it is revealed to you.

For we are God's handiwork,
created in Christ Jesus to do good works,
which God prepared in advance for us to do.
~ Ephesians 2:10

As you walk through the valley, people will come and go in your life. You are changing. Your life is changing. Your dreams and goals are changing. While some people will embrace your new life with you, others will not be able to. And that is okay! Push Through!

GRATITUDE

This may be a great time to grab a journal. It always helps me to put pen to paper. You may prefer the tablet or laptop for your thoughts. Whatever method you choose, start a Gratitude Journal. Go back and read this journal from time to time. You will be amazed at how your life changes after doing this journal.

Reflect on and be grateful for the whole life of your loved one: the tender moments shared, their strengths, the goodness of their total person. Write down everything you can think of about your loved one that you are thankful for. For example, I am thankful for my boyfriend's humor, his sense of adventure, and his love of dogs. Of course, there are so many other things I am thankful for when it comes to him.

Thank God for your loved one and the time you had together. That time is over. But that time together was part of a bigger plan. Worship God through the tears. God will give you strength. We don't understand why life happens as it does. We don't know why our loved one died by suicide. But we can trust God. He has the bigger picture in front of Him. We must have faith in this journey we are on.

It is God who arms me with strength
and keeps my way secure.
He makes my feet like the feet of a deer;
he causes me to stand on the heights.
He trains my hands for battle;
my arms can bend a bow of bronze.
You make your saving help my shield,
and your right hand sustains me;
your help has made me great.
You provide a broad path for my feet,
so that my ankles do not give way.
~ Psalm 18:32-36

Your loved one's life and their suicide are an integral part of who you are now. No one, nothing can take that away from you. Not even death itself. It will always be a chapter in your book. But it isn't the theme of the whole book.

Remember how your loved one lived their life, not how they died. Even when most people are so wrapped up in the "how" of the death, get away from those thoughts and concentrate on how your loved one lived their life: the person they were, the good times, and the moments that put a smile on your heart. Be thankful for the good of your loved one.

Everywhere we turn, we are surrounded by reminders of our loved one's life. It could be the rose bush she planted in the front yard. Or the wooden swing he made that sits on the front porch. Or a music cd they made for you. These can be strong triggers in the beginning of the grief. Over time, the magnitude of the triggers lessens. Maybe you won't cry every time you see their picture or when you hear a song on the radio.

In time, things will be better. Be patient with yourself. Let the reminders bring a smile to your heart, and not a tear to your eyes. Let them remind you to be thankful for your loved one – let them become gratitude triggers.

What if your loved one wasn't a "saint"? What if they messed up your life, in one way or another, prior to the suicide? Do you just pretend they were "perfect"? No. When we live in grace, we understand not only that we are forgiven by God for our sins, but that others are too. We don't need to ignore the "bad," but we don't need to dwell on it. When we have been wronged, we can forgive belatedly. Maybe life wasn't what it could have been with our loved one, but try to be thankful for what it was. Even in death, show grace to your loved one. And remember: we can go to God to ask forgiveness, since we can't go to our loved one.

Important advice given to me: people are going to say things about your loved one's past, or you may find out things you did not know about your loved one. Don't take it to heart. Remember the love and the good times you shared with your loved one. Forget the rest. Don't let things discovered after death taint the memory of your loved one.

There are so many ways to remember your loved one. Create a photo album of pictures and memories. Make a video from old pictures. Plant a tree. Climb a mountain. Do an activity that they loved to do. Participate in a memory walk or run. Write a song. Paint a picture. Sculpt. Volunteer at their favorite organization or help group.

Ask others to write letters about your loved one, and place them in a memory book. Make a memory quilt from your loved one's shirts, sweatshirts, and clothing. Make a teddy bear with old clothing. Visit places you enjoyed together.

Give away objects that were your loved one's to other people who cared about your loved one. Maybe a dear friend of your daughter would love to have her book collection. Or maybe your dad collected knives – give one to each grandchild.

Rejoice always, pray continually,
give thanks in all circumstances;
for this is God's will for you in Christ Jesus.
~ 1 Thessalonians 5:16-18

Be thankful for your loved one – that you had the chance to have them in your life, to love them, and to create memories with them. When we stay in a mindful expression of gratitude, we feel better. And what better way could we honor our loved one than by getting up and thanking God for them daily?

Be thankful for those who showed up for you during your grieving. It may be months later, but drop them a thank-you note or send them a text message or email. In whatever way you want to say "Thank you," just make sure you express gratitude to those who made a difference for you in your journey.

I have not stopped giving thanks for you,
remembering you in my prayers.
~ Ephesians 1:16

HOMEWORK

1 – Have you experienced being "stuck" in a certain phase of grief? When, how, and how long were you stuck? How can you Push Through?

2 – Make a list of what makes you feel strong/joyful/positive. Make another list of what makes you anxious/weak/sad. Look for patterns. What needs to change to help you Push Through?

3 – Find a funny movie, show, book, or hilarious friend – get to laughing. Journal about how laughing makes your soul feel.

4 – You are unique in your own passions, desires, purpose, and personality. What does the New You look like? Get to know yourself: the New You! Try to embrace the New You as an exciting chapter waiting to be written. Start writing it! Journal about this New You and the New Normal you're building. What has surprised you? Do others notice?

5 – Start a Gratitude Journal. Fill it up!

Practical Encouragement

How can you celebrate your loved one's life? Go do it!

Go for a walk and pray the entire walk with prayers of thanksgiving. It makes the walk go by fast.

Come up with three funny jokes that you can tell others to make them laugh!

WEEK 16

The Journey
Closure
After Grief

I am sure you never thought you would ever be on a grief journey that was the result of suicide. But here you are. You are still moving forward, one day at a time. You are Pushing Through, even when it feels like quicksand. I pray that, at this point, you have experienced healing or are continuing to heal, with your days becoming more bearable. I pray laughter has started to come back into your life. I pray God has given you peace and comfort. I pray that He has shown you the strength and courage that was inside you all along.

So, what now?

Oh no, another question . . .

This simple question also remains to be answered, like so many of our questions on this journey. Accept that the loss due to suicide will always be a part of you. You may not always get answers, or the answers may be different than expected. You will laugh again. You will live life with a more grateful heart.

You will remember your loved one, always. No method of death can take the memories we have of our loved one away from us. No method of death can take our love for our loved one away. No stigma, isolations, pain, or the roller coaster of emotions that have been experienced in this journey can take away the life we had with our loved one or the love we have for our loved one.

Do you feel like you got the closure you were expecting? Do you still find yourself disappointed? Have you seen the waves of this suicide loss grief ebb and flow, then realized that there is a season for everything?

There is a time for everything,
and a season for every activity under the heavens:
a time to be born and a time to die,
a time to plant and a time to uproot,
a time to kill and a time to heal,
a time to tear down and a time to build,
a time to weep and a time to laugh,
a time to mourn and a time to dance,
a time to scatter stones and a time to gather them,
a time to embrace and a time to refrain from embracing,
a time to search and a time to give up,
a time to keep and a time to throw away,
a time to tear and a time to mend,
a time to be silent and a time to speak,
a time to love and a time to hate,
a time for war and a time for peace.
~ Ecclesiastes 3:1-8

This journey has been totally out of your comfort zone. You have felt, seen, heard, acted, spoken, and expressed yourself in ways that you never would have imagined. You are courageous. You are a Warrior – a survivor!

Remember, there are no set rules for journeying through grief due to suicide loss. You've got to do it your way. Try not to compare your grief journey to anyone else's grief journey. And don't let someone who is also experiencing grief due to your loved one's death make you feel wrong because you are grieving differently than they are. You be you, and let them be them. We all journey this path in the way we must in order to survive.

Remember, no two grief journeys are alike. You may have lost someone you love before, to cancer or old age. And you question that the grief you are experiencing due to suicide is so much different. That is to be expected. Don't beat yourself up; there are no two grief journeys that look alike.

Go ahead and mentally prepare yourself with the fact that, in this grief journey, you will have aftershocks. Don't panic, as this is normal. You may repeat some of your grief steps. You will come back around. You will move forward, then take a step back, then move forward again. It's okay. It's your journey. There is no right or wrong on how this journey goes for you.

There is no timetable for this grief. Feelings come and go. Emotions come and go. There may be repeats of the different stages. You may experience flashes of anger or sadness. Be aware that triggers may represent unfinished business in regrets, guilt, and denial. Deal with the business. Push Through.

Just keep talking, as there is healing in talking. Keep journaling. It's therapeutic to put your thoughts on paper. It is amazing to go back a year later, read your journal, and see the steps you have made forward in this grief journey. You will see that you find it easier to talk about your loved one, talk about the memories you have of your loved one, and talk about the love you have for your loved one. You will feel more at peace.

Over time, you will discover that you talk less about your loved one. This is healing. It is okay to not talk about your loved one like you did in the beginning. Don't beat yourself up for not talking about them as much as you did in the beginning, or for not staying in the grief. It is healthy to Push Through.

Your loved one is part of you, not all of you. Your loved one will always be a part of you. Don't let grief turn into your sole identity.

I know you feel lost since your loved one is gone, but grief is not the New You.

We never forget our loved one, but we do Push Through the grief. It may still seem hard to believe that you will Push Through where you are right now. But look where you have come from. Amazing! This, too, shall pass . . .

Break my heart,
Oh break it again,
so I can love more fully.
~ Rumi

Have you come to the point when you feel you have more love in your heart than you did before your loved one died? More compassion? Or are you still numb? Empty?

It may seem hard to believe or even understand, but you will emerge from this grieving process with a renewed spirit, restored health, and new empathy for others. Your heart will be so much bigger than you ever imagined it could be! Your perspective has changed, and your heart of compassion is larger than it has ever been. Whatever you have discovered about your heart, show it to the world!

Do you want to be the exclamation mark for your loved one's life? Go do something that will represent the ending punctuation mark for your loved one's life. I am sure their life did not end the way you had hoped for them, just as their life didn't end the way they had imagined it would. So, go give their life an exclamation mark! Celebrate them! Have their name be remembered in a positive way. Get creative. Maybe honor them at their favorite place to be, or with their friends, or through a favorite charity. Create a scholarship in their memory. Accomplish the goal they had wanted for themselves, like learning to play the guitar.

You will experience what I call "Tender Days" – anniversaries, birthdays, weddings, family events, special days, and holidays. These could be days when you wish they were there with you, or a special day that you had shared with them. Get with your family and/or friends and create new traditions on these Tender Days. Light a candle in memory of your loved one and set it on the table when a family meal is shared. Go to their favorite restaurant and order their favorite meal. Visit their grave and have a long talk with them. Release balloons. Plant a tree that blooms, a fragrant plant, or a bush.

What did your loved one like? Stray animals? Helping the elderly? Cooking? Go volunteer in your loved one's memory, at their favorite charitable cause. Some examples would be to volunteer at an animal shelter, go read to children at the library, or get involved in church. Get involved in a small group where you are not inundated with the word suicide – maybe a group that likes to go hunting or fishing, or a group that likes to travel or enjoys concerts. Don't get upset with yourself about how you handle these Tender Days.

Hopefully, you have made connections in your support group and feel safe and connected with them. Your support group will help you integrate back into the world. The people in your support group become your people and your tribe. Your immediate support group can be a group that you meet with once a week, or just a few close friends or family members. Whatever your own support group looks like, that is fine. It is yours, and it works for you. No rules in this grief journey.

It is important in your healing journey to establish structure. A routine gives you purpose and a sense of accomplishment. Get up at the same time every day. Go to bed at the same time every day. Make a To Do List. Check it off daily. Keep a visible calendar. Check the days off. I prefer paper over electronic; you do what works for you.

There is a country song by Gary Allan that has stuck with me through my journey and gives me hope: *"Every storm runs out of rain, just like every dark night turns to day."* There will be daybreak. The sun will shine. And my light will shine again. Your light will shine again, too.

It is possible for your tragedy to turn into a masterpiece of triumph. One day, you will see that your grief has turned to glory! Be hopeful and keep your eyes on the next step in front of you.

Survival of this suicide loss grief journey is a place of memories and tears because you miss your loved one. Survival of this suicide loss grief journey finishes out as reclaimed joy and hope. Survival is not moving on and forgetting your loved one. Survival is when you begin to look forward to life again. Keep Pushing Through. Let this experience turn you from a piece of coal into a diamond.

> *"Forget the former things;*
> *do not dwell on the past.*
> *See, I am doing a new thing!*
> *Now it springs up; do you not perceive it?*
> *I am making a way in the wilderness*
> *and streams in the wasteland."*
> ~ Isaiah 43:18-19

As much as we want to, we cannot undo suicide. But in healing, you can go on with your life in a way that is healthier and more creative. Your life will be more productive. You will begin seeing things for what they truly are. In healing and over time, memories become pleasant things, not bringing anger, guilt, or depression any longer.

There will always be a remnant of pain, but don't let it overshadow your joy. Don't let the method of death of your loved one define who you are. Remember: how your loved one died is not who they were.

Regardless of what we face, the outcome will always be for His glory. Keep your focus on Him. Find ways in your grief to glorify God.

So whether you eat or drink or whatever you do,
do it all for the glory of God.
~ 1 Corinthians 10:31

I know and believe my future is bigger than my past. I have HOPE. I have open eyes and an open heart, which leads to a new vision and new possibilities. Having a fresh hope leads to new dreams. Even though it seems scary, open your heart up to dream again. If we forget to remember, we forget to be thankful. Push Through to a new life, a new future, and new hope.

Brothers and sisters,
I do not consider myself yet to have taken hold of it.
But one thing I do:
Forgetting what is behind and straining toward what is ahead,
I press on toward the goal to win the prize
for which God has called me heavenward in Christ Jesus.
~ Philippians 3:13-14

See, the former things have taken place,
and new things I declare . . ."
~ Isaiah 42:9a

Whenever guilt, fear, or condemnation begin to rise in our hearts, we can be certain it is the devil seeking to hold us back from fully embracing the future God has promised us. The devil wants control over God's children, so beware: the devil tries hard to keep us distracted so we do not stay close to God. And I am pretty

213

sure you have grown closer in your walk with God during this grief journey. Just beware!

You intended to harm me, but God intended it for good
to accomplish what is now being done, the saving of many lives.
~ Genesis 50:20

We have choices. We have free will. In this suicide loss grief, we all have to choose to journey on. Our timing is not God's timing. God's timing is perfect. Accept His timing. At this point of your journey, focus on getting healthy, healing, and recovering. God will bring it all together. Trust Him.

You will know the Lord better at the end of this journey than you did before the suicide of your loved one. If the Lord Jesus Christ wasn't already a part of your daily routine through Bible study, prayer, meditation, and worship, then it's not too late. God allows U-turns. Seek Him.

As you get your energy back and you are out of your grief fog, just say YES. Go do something you have always wanted to do. Be adventurous. Step out of your comfort zone. Discover your new self. It may help to make room in your life for something new. Buy a new pair of walking shoes. Plant a new rose bush in the yard. Go do something you don't normally do for yourself, like spending a day at the spa. Or take on a new heart of gratitude: send all of your closest friends a personalized note of thanksgiving.

To move on in this journey, accept the decision your loved one made. Do not be destroyed by it. You may always be angry and confused that your loved one chose to leave by suicide, but you have no more time to lose to the grief. A year to 18 months of constant grief is normal and healthy. The journey of suicide loss grief is constantly moving forward and changing. Be okay with how this looks for you and your life.

Grief changes shape, but it never ends.
~ Keanu Reeves

As the intensity of the grief diminishes, promise is stirred within you of unexpected possibilities and options. This is hope. Embrace the hope.

I am the keeper of my boyfriend's memory, so I must be whole. I could not have stopped him. I chose love. I chose to love again. I chose forgiveness. I chose laughter. I chose to enjoy the freedom to live again. My boyfriend made his choice. I have made mine: to live a full, rich, joy-filled life, and to be excited about the potential of my future.

Turn away from the guilt and shame. Always forgive your loved one and yourself. Respect others. Respect yourself. Love others. Love yourself. Remember, love always wins.

Look forward! The rearview mirror is small, and the front windshield is much bigger. If you spend all of your time looking in the rearview mirror, you will not be able to move forward, and you will probably wreck the car. You glance back in the rearview mirror from time to time, to see where you have been – to see the dust roll off your tires. Stay focused. Keep your eyes ahead. The future, as with the front windshield, is big.

Believe me when I say that time does make the pain lesson. Look forward to those days ahead: the days with less pain! In the tragedy (our pain), God performs a miracle (our healing), which leads to our mission (our testimony). Our mess turns into a message. Our test turns into a testimony. I have learned that I have a new message to share with others because of this suicide loss grief journey. And I am excited to share it with others so they can visually see the healing that God has done in me.

Keep the faith that God is working this out for us. Good will be the end result. Weeping may stay for the night, but rejoicing comes in the morning.

> *. . . joy comes with the morning.*
> ~ Psalm 30:5b (ESV)

Envision that your life is a tapestry. It is made up of all kinds of threads, all woven together and intertwined. One of those strings may not be such a pretty color alone. For example, diarrhea-green is not a pretty color. But when you weave in this ugly thread, it becomes a part of the beautiful tapestry.

Our tragedy of losing our loved one to suicide is an ugly thread, but it is a part of our beautiful tapestry. Our loved one is a much more beautiful thread: it is a vibrant, energetic, lovely piece of thread. We have more of our loved one's thread than the suicide thread in our tapestry. Wow! The ugly and beautiful threads become part of our fabric – what we are made up of. The ugly colors make the beautiful colors that much more beautiful! Your tapestry is an absolutely stunning tapestry! Show it to the world!

HOMEWORK

1 – Can you look back and see where you have come from? Go back over your journal and see where you have healed.

2 – How are you dealing with the Tender Days?

3 – Continue to talk. Who is your 2 a.m. friend? Write them a letter of appreciation.

4 – Write down your goals in your New Normal. What do you want to come out of your journey with? Without?

5 – How are you going to end this part of the journey with a punctuation mark for your loved one? How will you honor your loved one going forward in a life-giving/loving way?

Practical Encouragement

Create a sanctuary just for you – a place to read, pray, journal, be quiet, just think, and be comfortable. No clutter. Light a candle. Try to spend some time every day in your sanctuary.

Try something new once a month. Journal about these new experiences. Let each new adventure build a new habit of gratitude.

SURVIVING TENDER DAYS
AND THE HOLIDAYS

~ Days to be considered: birthdays, anniversaries, graduation dates, "firsts" days, "special memories" days, previous vacations, "shared memories" days, death date, July 4th, Thanksgiving, Christmas, New Year's, Easter, Valentine's Day.

~ Recognize that the Tender Days and holidays are going to be tough – emotionally, relationally, physically, spiritually. Accept that there will be struggles.

~ Don't fight the added emotions; accept them. Don't hold back. Don't force an emotion based on others' expectations of you.

~ Set realistic expectations for yourself, not others. Know your limitations. You can only control you, not others. So, let go of the expectations you have for others.

~ You or others in the family may or may not want to continue with some traditions. Be open to talking this over. Be open to doing something different. Start new traditions.

~ Decide if you want to be with family and/or friends, or just go away and be alone for the Tender Days or holidays. Maybe try a mixture of time with others and time alone. You decide what works for you.

~ If it is comforting to talk about your loved one, do so. Share with your family and friends that it is okay to talk about your loved one. But if it is not comfortable, share with family and friends that you do not want to talk about your loved one, or for them to talk about your loved one around you. We have to step up at this time and share our expectations. The "Catch-22 Cards" will come into play at this time. You may waver back and forth and back: *"Yes, talk about my loved one." "No, don't talk about my loved one." "Only*

219

talk about happy memories, not their death." "Let's talk about our first or our lasts." Back and forth, up and down, like a seesaw. It is okay!

EMOTIONAL AMBUSHES

Expect emotional ambushes. What is an emotional ambush? A trigger creates an emotional ambush. The trigger takes place and backs you into an emotional corner that was unexpected. Triggers can be activities, traditions, songs, memories, tastes, smells, sights, or anything that reminds you of your loved one. They will happen, and the unknown of when or how can be frustrating and could even create another emotion: anxiety. Expecting triggers will help lessen the "ambush" factor.

LONELINESS

A Tender Day or holiday without your loved one will heighten feelings of loneliness. You may be surrounded by people. You may be busy. But your loved one's presence is still missed. There is a part of you that is missing. Recognize this loneliness, accept this situation, and look for healthy and productive ways to ease that lonely feeling. (Ex: get connected to others, give back to the community, volunteer, reach out to someone who understands your grief)

DO NOT NUMB THE PAIN

Numbing pain isn't always negative, but most times, it is. Initially, we may numb just to be able to Push Through a moment or feeling. We may find that we are putting in longer hours at work, participating in too many social/volunteer activities, engaging in sexual activity or a new romantic relationship because it "feels good" to escape the emotional stress, spending money on things we don't need, overindulging in alcohol or drugs, or pursuing any increased behavior or action to help forget the pain. This is not the answer. If you find yourself in this situation, please seek the help that will be most beneficial to you.

WRITE A GRIEF LETTER

A grief letter can be written in various situations. You may write one for others who inquire about how you are doing. In it, you will describe how you feel, your experiences, and your expectations or desires. You can share what is comforting and what is not comforting, as well as a list of specific, practical needs other people can help with. Keep copies handy for any social events you may attend. You may also want to write a grief letter to your loved one whom you miss and who is not there for the Tender Day or holiday.

HAVE A PLAN

In advance, make a plan for the Tender Day or holiday. Decide whether or not to continue the traditions that are so hard without your loved one. Create a straightforward yet flexible plan for what and how much you want to do. If you have 15 events to be a part of, know which are a priority and which are not. If you need to skip certain events, it is okay. Communicate your plan with your loved ones and friends.

Remember, you can't duplicate past special days or holidays. And every special day or holiday from here on out will not be a cookie cutter reproduction of this one. Do try to have repeated traditions, but also be flexible as the years pass and more and more healing takes place.

HONOR YOUR LOVED ONE

There are so many ways to honor your loved one. Burn a candle at the dinner table. Have everyone at family gatherings or social events share a happy memory of your loved one. Volunteer at a pet shelter if your loved one had a passion for pets. Plant a tree in your yard in their memory. Buy an ornament for the Christmas tree that reminds you of your loved one. The money you would have spent on your loved one for the special day or holiday can now be donated in their memory at their favorite charity.

HELP YOUR CHILDREN SURVIVE
THE TENDER DAYS AND HOLIDAYS

Are there children in your life who are also grieving? TALK with them ahead of time about expectations, feelings, and traditions. INCLUDE them in the special day or holiday planning, such as putting up lights outdoors, going to a relative's home, cooking a meal, etc. HELP THEM EXPRESS what they are feeling in positive ways like coloring, sculpting, exercise, or a favorite activity of theirs. It is important in their healing to keep them included

TAKE CARE OF YOURSELF

Be intentional in taking care of yourself. Make time for yourself.

Emotional/Mental Health – Set aside time for reflection so you can process the new emotions and stressors of the season. It may help to write down these feelings in a Tender Days Journal. Have a friend listen to you, or see your counselor. There is healing in talking.

Physical Health – Get enough rest, make smart eating choices, and exercise. Go for a walk! Get a massage, see the chiropractor, get a manicure/pedicure.

Spiritual Health – Make this a season of renewal and focus. Get involved at church. Pray. Meditate. Listen to God by getting alone and being quiet.

DON'T OVERBURDEN YOURSELF

During seasonal holidays, decorate as much as you want to. Instead of sending cards, send a personal note – or nothing at all. Don't be surprised if this may alarm others, since this is not what you typically do. Cook/bake less than you used to. (Don't be surprised if you are told that your family misses your famous dessert at the family gathering.) Don't stress over gift-giving. You may decide to do charitable donations instead of the typical, tangible gift-giving.

As for other Tender Days, don't put pressure on yourself to do as you have always done for birthdays, anniversaries, graduations, or other days when you would usually put in extra effort. Do what you can handle comfortably. It's okay to ask for help with typical "special day" expectations. You are experiencing a new normal. And you get to make those choices as to what works best for you.

SOCIAL EVENTS

Be intentional about balancing time alone and time spent with others. Special days and holidays can be overly demanding on your time. And now that you are trying to Push Through your grief, the demands may be more than usually overwhelming.

With Others – Talk about your loved one, share memories, and safely express your grief while feeling overwhelmed by difficult emotions. It's okay to admit you are hurting when asked. Spend time with safe people, not those who lean toward unhealthy vices. If it helps, ahead of the Tender Days or holidays, make a list of your "safe" people.

Be prepared for questions that may be asked. Beforehand, script those responses out. Remember, people are going to say hurtful things and make "odd" comments to you, without meaning to cause you pain. Show grace. People usually don't mean to cause harm. Your tribe just wants you to be happy and without pain.

Alone – Explore the latest feelings and thoughts. Avoid temptations to numb any pain with drugs, alcohol, destructive behavior, overspending, overeating, etc. Get in a private, peaceful, and quiet place. Have your favorite "God loves me" affirming scripture written down and handy so you can reference this when you need a positive lift.

Holiday Invitations – You don't have to say Yes to every invite. It's okay to say No, and don't feel guilty about last-minute decisions not to go to an event. You have to do what is healthy for you.

Plan to stay at least thirty minutes at the events you do attend. Give it a try. Drive yourself so you can leave if you need to, or go with someone so they can run interference for you if needed. Have a plan if you need to leave the room to cry or just to catch your breath. Just be you.

GRATITUDE

Be thankful for the memories with your loved one. Reflect on those. Share them with others. It may help to write down all of the "gifts" your loved one gave to you over the years. For example, the gift of giving you a hug every time they saw you, or of calling you when they arrived at their destination. Or it could be that scarf that was a Christmas gift many years ago. Or the special Valentine's Day card.

Make a list in your Tender Days Journal of the things you are thankful for. (Ex: time you had with your loved one, special memories shared, their legacy, what you learned from your loved one, and just everyday things to be thankful for)

EASING THE PAIN

It may help you to find ways to ease the pain during the special days or holidays. Consider spending the special days or holidays with someone who is alone or who might need you. Go be with family or friends. Volunteer. Adopt a family. Make a monetary donation in your loved one's memory.

It does get easier, even when it feels like it won't. There is HOPE amid grief.

Be intentional about surrounding yourself with those who will support and care for you through your grief process ("safe" people).

Remember, the anticipation is sometimes worse than the actual event. After the special day or holiday, you may even experience a letdown, along with guilt, regret, or frustrations. Talk, see your counselor, get together with a friend, or do whatever helps you when you are in an unhealthy place mentally.

There is no "right" way to handle the holidays, special days, anniversaries, or birthdays. You decide. You can even change your mind in the middle of a special day or holiday event if the event is too stressful. What doesn't work can be done differently the next time.

We never "get over it", but we do Push Through!

MOTHER'S/FATHER'S DAY AFTER LOSING A CHILD

The first Mother's Day/Father's Day without your child will be the absolute hardest. And the ones to follow will also be "Tender Days" (my term for those special days in the year that are so much harder after losing our loved one to suicide) for you as well. This day may be bittersweet, full of both beautiful memories and then moments of regret or *"what if"*'s and *"if I would have"*'s. There may be renewed feelings of guilt, shame, anger, bitterness, and other previous grief emotions.

What do you say when someone asks you how many children you have? *"I have/gave birth to/adopted three, but one has passed away."* It is healthy to say just that. Then, if the person doesn't know your journey, they may ask how the one child passed away. The answer is whatever you choose. One option is *"My child died from mental illness"* or *"as a result of PTSD."*

Then there is the awkward moment when someone might say, *"At least you have another child/ren."* What? Our love does not end just because our child is gone. And just because our child passes away doesn't mean they never existed. Mother's Day/Father's Day is a time when we want to be honored for all of our children, and not ignore the fact that we were a parent to a child that passed away from suicide. Yet, society treats the death differently if it was suicide. Why? That is one question that will never get answered.

Mothers/Fathers do not forget their children. Maybe you have felt you needed to be silent about your child because of how they died, or simply because they are not here any longer and it's hard to even say their name out loud. I encourage you to speak your child's name. Let their name cross your lips. Talk about your child with your "safe" people. There is healing in talking.

You can answer and respond to the questions or comments from others in whatever way you like. There is no shame that your child passed away. And there is no shame that your child died by suicide.

Some people may be afraid to address the day with you, so they might say nothing. Remember: whether they say something hurtful or hurt you by saying nothing at all, people that care about you want you to be happy and do not mean to cause harm. I don't think most humans want to go out and purposefully hurt others. People just don't know what to say. This is a good time to practice compassion and forgiveness to others.

Mother's Day/Father's Day may bring about feelings of guilt that you failed your child. *Why else would they take their life?* This isn't true. There is no failure on your part, and you did not play a part in their decision. No one is perfect – you or your child. Parenting is not easy, and children do not come with instruction manuals. Take it easy on yourself – especially on Mother's Day/Father's Day.

I am sure your thoughts will be on Mother's Day/Father's Day long before the day actually arrives. The anticipation of a Tender Day can create more anxiety than the actual day itself. The unknown of how you will feel and what will happen that day can be overwhelming; will you fall apart, be grateful with pleasant memories, be at peace, or feel nothing at all?

At this tender time, you may need to go see your counselor or speak with your accountability partner. There are no set rules on grief, especially when you lose your child. It isn't natural for a child to pass before its parents. With suicide, which is also an unnatural process of death, it seems that the grief is even more compounded. Suicide – unnatural. Child dying before parent – unnatural. Traumatic event – unnatural.

As in the suicide loss grief process, there is no right or wrong in how you do Mother's Day/Father's Day. You must do it your way, no doubt. If you have other children, you may decide that spending this day with them is beneficial. Or those children may live elsewhere and can't be with you on Mother's Day/Father's Day. You will have to do Mother's Day/Father's Day the way you feel is best for you.

There will be others in your life that are not sure how you want Mother's Day/Father's Day to go. They may be afraid to ask you about that day. Try to find a way to express what you need and want. You may have to write it down and give that written need or want to your loved ones. Sometimes the right words just do not come easily when speaking, but if you can put pen to paper, it flows better and you can express yourself without worrying that you may fall apart emotionally.

I suggest making up a "Catch-22 Card" to hand to others this week, depending on how you feel. Maybe make up two different cards – one that says *"I want to talk about my child as Mother's Day/Father's Day approaches"* and another that says *"I do not wish to talk about losing my child and Mother's Day/Father's Day"*. Word it the way your heart leads you to. This will help others know how you want to be treated at this precious time.

Especially on Mother's Day/Father's Day, we can choose to celebrate the life our child had and lived. Don't focus on the method of death. Go do something positive in your child's memory. Run a race, start a college scholarship, plant a tree, volunteer at an animal shelter, build a book share house, or go do an activity your child enjoyed. The possibilities are endless as you celebrate your child. This may also help you with the sadness that can creep up on you leading up to and even after Mother's Day/Father's Day.

Make it a day of purpose. Plan ahead. You are learning what your triggers are. You know who your tribe is. You know what gives you peace. You know if staying busy or remaining quiet is best for you on Mother's Day/Father's Day. You do this day the way that is most healthy for you.

After Mother's Day/Father's Day, you may feel let down that the day wasn't like previous Mother's Days/Father's Days. You may be disappointed that it didn't go as you wanted. That is okay. As you Push Through in your grief journey, you have a choice to make: stay stuck or heal.

Each year, your Mother's Day/Father's Day will be different, just as each of our days in this grief journey is different. Be open to doing things differently as you Push Through. Each Mother's Day/Father's Day that passes will be a little less draining, exhausting, and taxing on your emotions, mental state, and physical being. It is okay to keep Pushing Through this grief. Healing does happen. Don't feel guilty that your grief is not as deeply expressed as time marches on.

You will always be their Mother/Father. Take this Mother's Day/Father's Day to remember happy times together. Remember their birth and their early years of firsts. Give thanks for this child and the time you had together on this earth. Go for a walk, get your journal out, talk with a friend, or choose whatever way you want to get the feelings out. Do something in their memory on Mother's Day/Father's Day!

You are ALWAYS their Mother/Father! Nothing can take that away!

Made in the USA
Coppell, TX
15 August 2021